Praise for *Go Fo*

In this compelling book, Rosie Yeo reminds us of why strategy days often fall short of expectations and systematically provides us with a practical roadmap for ensuring our work in developing strategy is bold, inclusive and impactful. I particularly like her powerful concept of 'everyday alchemy' and its ability to totally transform our strategic discussions.

Dr David Cooke, Adjunct Professor, UTS Business School; Chair, UN Global Compact Network Australia; Director, ESG Advisory

Go for Bold is a fantastic book for both facilitators and participants in the strategic planning process. Rosie captures inspiration from real-life examples and, combined with her know-how and practical experience at a Board level, challenges the reader to break free of their traditional strategy templates. A must-read for anyone wanting to move beyond their traditional approach to strategy and reset their processes for a future of dynamic strategic planning.

Carolyn Miller, advertising and communications strategist; *Gruen* panellist; Director/Founder, The Honeycomb Effect

Rosie has complemented her great skill as a strategic planning facilitator with this meticulously researched and highly readable book on this important subject. It has been my experience that strategic planning and the successful execution of those plans too often fall short of both expectation and what is possible. This book, full of real-world examples, will assist any senior executive contemplating better strategic planning for their enterprise.

Major General (Ret'd) Duncan Lewis AO DSC CSC, Chair, Painaustralia; Former Director-General, Australian Security Intelligence Organisation; Former Secretary, Department of Defence

Go for Bold provides a wealth of real-life stories and quality advice for leaders in how best to fulfil their roles in developing or reviewing strategy. An entertaining and thought-provoking read for every Board Chair, Director and organisational leader.

Wendy Machin, Non-executive Director (Heritage Bank, Golf Australia) and Chair (Reflections Holiday Parks); Former President, NRMA; Chair, Customer Owned Banking Association (COBA); NSW Minister for Consumer Affairs

In business, the only way to stand out is to be bold, with courage, conviction and deep focus. Rosie has written a book that is a guide to big-thinking but committed execution. The world is full of overnight success stories that could have been – perhaps *Go for Bold* will give you the insights you will need for the 'long road' to success.

Naomi Simson, entrepreneur

GO FOR BOLD

GO FOR BOLD

HOW TO CREATE
POWERFUL
STRATEGY
IN UNCERTAIN TIMES

ROSIE YEO

MAJOR
STREET

For Imogen, Lily and Ian

 First published in 2022 by Major Street Publishing Pty Ltd
info@majorstreet.com.au | +61 421 707 983 | majorstreet.com.au

 A catalogue record for this book is available
from the National Library of Australia

Printed book ISBN: 978-1-9226113-0-7
Ebook ISBN: 978-1-9226113-1-4

The nine rules on pages 75-76 are from "Never Take a Right Turn at Albuquerque" from
CHUCK AMUCK: THE LIFE AND TIMES OF AN ANIMATED CARTOONIST by
Chuck Jones. Copyright © 1989 by Chuck Jones Enterprises, Inc. Reprinted by permission
of Farrar, Straus and Giroux. All Rights Reserved.

Cover design by Tess McCabe
Internal design by Production Works
Printed in Australia by Printed in Australia by Ovato, an Accredited ISO AS/NZS
14001:2004 Environmental Management System Printer.

10 9 8 7 6 5 4 3 2 1

Contents

Introduction

It's late on a Friday night in early March 2020. Glenn Keys, founder and Executive Chairman of Aspen Medical, is sitting with his chief financial officer in their sleek, industrial-style Canberra headquarters. Open on the screen in front of them are the company's bank accounts and Glenn's personal accounts, and the CFO is waiting on Glenn's decision:

> 'I can make this deposit, but I have to drain every single account. We will have nothing left.'

Most of us had no idea at this stage how the emerging global pandemic would impact the world, but Aspen Medical, expert in delivering healthcare in the toughest situations around the globe, was ahead of the curve in understanding the scale of the challenge. Sourcing personal protective equipment (PPE) for the safety of healthcare staff and the community was going to be a major priority, and the contest for supplies was already fierce.

Glenn had the opportunity to confirm an order worth hundreds of millions of dollars for PPE on behalf of the Australian Government, but there was no time to lose. Without payment of a sizeable deposit by midnight, the order would lapse, and there were a lot of other countries in the wings desperate to secure PPE.

The speed of the deal meant there was no contract in place. Glenn had received an email from a high-level government contact confirming the government's request to obtain supplies, but there was no other paperwork and Aspen Medical would have to pay the full deposit.

Glenn considered what was at stake:

'If this goes wrong, it's the end of the company – but I am confident it's not going to go wrong.'

He made the decision:

'Okay, pay the lot.'

It was a long Friday night. Once the money had left the accounts, he headed home and drank a glass of wine with his wife Mel while they waited. A call from a government adviser at 11.30 p.m. heightened his anxiety, as more questions were being asked. It appeared that the deal may still not yet be formally approved.

Fifteen minutes after midnight, Glenn received a call confirming that the government paperwork had been signed.

Glenn told me he shocked the government adviser (and his wife, who could hear the conversation) by saying:

'"I've got to tell you, I almost wet myself when I got your initial call this evening." My wife was standing there going: "Why would you say that?" And I said, "Because it's true. I wanted to let them know how personal this was."'

I've been privileged to work with Glenn on a few projects over the past few years and I've learnt a lot from observing him identify and analyse opportunities, weigh up risks and how to mitigate them, and make bold decisions. He highlights the importance of open thinking (not narrowing in too quickly on one option), careful analysis and clarity before making decisions.

What a pandemic revealed about our approach to strategy

Looking back, it's extraordinary how nimbly we responded to the global and local crises caused by the COVID-19 pandemic. Health services rolled out rapid COVID-19 testing sites across populations; the acceleration of telehealth consultations saw Australia's Health Minister boast that a ten-year plan for telehealth had been implemented within ten days;[1] and major organisations transitioned to working from home in a matter of weeks.

Our experience in 2020 and 2021 showed us we could be more adaptable, even creative, in a crisis. We were forced into making faster decisions, changing the way we do things and even what we do.

We threw some planning structures out the window

Some people loved the freedom that the pandemic offered in regard to planning. Herman Spruit, a London-based management consultant at Bain & Company, saw some surprising upsides when the pandemic disrupted fixed planning cycles:

> 'When CEOs describe what they liked during lockdown, they basically say, "Without our planning systems, it all became so simple. Some meetings were about doing stuff. We just sorted out jobs to do, agreed on a playbook and just did it. And in other meetings, we understood the need to invent. We formed the right teams and started experimenting.""[2]

Our horizons narrowed and we lost confidence in planning for the long term

When I'm creating strategic plans with organisations, we normally focus on a three-year horizon, or sometimes five years, or even up to twenty years ahead. But in 2020 and 2021, many of my corporate, non-profit and association clients were saying the same thing:

> 'We just need to survive the next six to twelve months; we'll worry about the future later!'

While some welcomed the opportunity to shake things up and abandon the strictures of rigid planning cycles, I also saw many organisations lose confidence in their ability to plan for the long term. In many ways, that made perfect sense. We all saw the ground rules shift constantly, with restrictions, border closures and ongoing uncertainty preventing many organisations from looking ahead with confidence. People and organisations suffered from the immediate impacts of unprecedented lockdowns, and months into the pandemic many organisations still could not see the way through.

Government financial support and temporary changes to corporate insolvency provisions cushioned the immediate impact of the pandemic. (The number of companies entering external administration in Australia actually decreased by 47 per cent for the year to May 2021 compared with the prior year.[3]) However, long-term concerns remain about the viability of many organisations that have struggled through two tough years.

Now, we feel more uncertain

In Australia, we were fortunate to avoid the massive toll of death and illness experienced by many countries during the first year of the pandemic. Nonetheless, through 2021, we were living with uncertainty. For much of the year our population was largely unvaccinated, our largest cities entered long lockdowns and we remained locked off from the world through border closures, without a clear timetable for reopening. So, it's not surprising that people continued to avoid those long-term discussions.

But here's another perspective: there's always been uncertainty about the future – always. We've never been able to control everything; we just used to think we could!

The jolt into the unknown through the COVID-19 pandemic has been a sobering reminder that circumstances are always shifting. Our operating environment, our customers and our own organisations change over time, sometimes abruptly. That doesn't mean we give up on strategy, though – it underlines the importance of learning how to be strategic together.

We need to reach shared, powerful agreements about our long game, because that is how our organisations will maintain the resilience to keep moving forward despite upheaval.

Bold strategy is uncomfortable

Look up 'boldness' in your choice of dictionary and you'll find it defined as a willingness to take risks, an indication of confidence, courage, even fearlessness. Look at many organisations today and those words may not be the first descriptors that come to mind! (We look at why this is in chapter 1.)

Creating groundbreaking strategy is not easy. We must challenge our ideas of what's possible, what's likely and what's important. We need to choose to do new things, and sometimes to choose to stop doing things we've always done. Sometimes, we need to go out on a limb.

But when we create big plans together, we understand and feel ownership of the story and responsibility for achieving the outcome. We can make braver decisions because we see the risks within the context of our full story.

Our primary objective as team leaders, organisational leaders and aspiring business owners is to set the right path forward. The strategies most likely to succeed are the plans designed together with those who know your organisation best – your people – and this doesn't happen by itself. The purpose of this book is to show how to harness your potential and your team's potential to create more powerful strategy: how to bring to life bold plans that create positive impact.

This book offers you a new approach to designing your future, focused on how you can inspire others to think differently, work through challenging issues constructively and ultimately become committed to a shared future for your organisation.

This is not just about how you run one strategy meeting or one offsite retreat. Rather, we ask the question, 'How can you build your collective strategic mindset?' In other words, how can you and your team look further ahead, think smarter and make better decisions for long-term benefit?

The tools and ideas in this book are as relevant for a small business as they are for larger organisations; they will help you surface smarter, more ambitious ideas together and be bold enough to bring them to life.

This book sets out three steps to creating bolder strategy.

In Part I, we focus on the importance of strategy and highlight some of the ways we hinder ourselves when trying to create and implement bold plans. I introduce you to the concept of strategy alchemy, where blending together key elements can produce something of greater value – bold plans for future success.

In Part II, we work through the three key elements we need to blend to create bolder, more powerful strategy: creativity, clarity and consensus. These are essential whether you're going it alone, leading a small team or leading a large organisation.

Part III focuses on how you and your team can unleash your own power, helping you get the most out of your big strategy meetings and your ongoing strategic conversations.

Not another strategy day!

My shift to becoming a professional facilitator and strategy alchemist was initially sparked by frustration. As a company director and public affairs strategist, I came to dread many of the planning sessions I was required to attend. They seemed so rigid, filled with jargon, and by the end of the day everyone just wanted to leave the room as quickly as possible.

Sitting on a national regulatory Board, I watched consultants roll out fixed templates for strategic planning year after year. It seemed like the main objective was to ensure that this Board filled in every box with the same decisions as 14 other related Boards. New ideas or alternative approaches were treated as inconveniences that would interrupt the schedule and mess up the pre-drafted report.

As a public affairs adviser, I was designing strategy for clients all the time, but I was so busy proving the value of my input (like every self-respecting consultant!) that I didn't focus on the potential for group insights and debate to enrich the ideas and bring strategy to life.

With these lessons in mind, I made it my mission to change the way people talk about the future, to supercharge those conversations about future strategies and long-term public policy and create powerful change.

I have been lucky enough to spend the past decade working with corporate, association, non-profit and government clients leading those important conversations. I come home from every session I facilitate second-guessing my approach and analysing what happened in the room and beyond: how did new ideas surface; how was genuine consensus reached; how did things change? My observations have sparked repeated dives into the literature and ongoing testing of new ideas and approaches on my inspiring client guinea pigs. (A huge thanks to all my clients for allowing me to share in their most important conversations.)

This book offers proven, easy-to-use techniques for having your ongoing conversations about the future – but most importantly, I hope you will walk away with a changed mindset about every strategy discussion that you lead or participate in.

The way we talk about the future changes the future we create, so our conversations about strategy matter.

We have more capacity than we think to change the world and our place in it. But unimaginative, tick-the-box approaches to planning produce unimaginative, uninspiring future plans.

Every strategy discussion is a high-stakes conversation, because strategy determines our potential to succeed or fail. One-off strategy days are important, but your conversations throughout the year are equally so.

The pandemic has proven we can be adaptable, even creative in a crisis. Now, let's get more ambitious. Let's apply that creativity and our ability to pull together to start boldly planning for longer-term success, despite uncertainty. Let's change our mindset to become more strategic and more focused on our long game, despite ongoing upheaval. Changing the way we approach strategy:

· enables new ideas to surface
· maps a better pathway that's more likely to succeed
· inspires people to genuinely commit to change.

My dad always says, 'It's about sharing the journey'. Strategy is about making progress over time. The keys in this book will help you aim higher, get there faster and, most importantly, bring people with you on your chosen path. Now more than ever we need to be bold, so let's be bolder together in mapping our path forward – an uncertain future demands it.

PART I
STRATEGY IS
NOT FOR WIMPS
(WHY WE NEED
BOLDNESS)

IF STRATEGY WERE a character in an action movie, I think it would be the nerdy, underacknowledged teen who quietly creates a brilliant new algorithm and surprises everyone when he or she steps up to bravely save the day.

The word 'strategy' is thrown around a lot, but not everyone is sure what it means or what it does. I once heard a podcast interviewer asking a health expert, 'How do you use coffee strategically in your day?' As a morning coffee addict, I understand the intent of this question – but strategy isn't about the quick hit. It's about setting up your long game.

The mention of strategy often induces a yawn or a yelp. People see it as too hard, too boring or someone else's job. They forget that when the right strategies are brought to life, they can change organisations and lives for the better. So it's worth getting strategy right.

In this first part of the book, I break down what strategy is and why it's important for us to become better at creating it. We need to confidently create and implement the best strategy so that our teams, our organisations and even our communities can survive and thrive.

It's challenging to plan a future, particularly in times of uncertainty, but we need to do it, and as robustly as we can. Understanding the sources of powerful strategy will help unlock our collective power to bring our best futures to life.

Chapter 1
Death by framework
(and other problems with our approach to strategy)

'Colour'; 'movement'; 'soaring ambition'; 'death-defying feats'.

Have you used any of these words to describe your experiences with strategic planning?

Possibly not – and that's something this book aims to change. These descriptions are apt, however, for the performances staged by global theatrical phenomenon Cirque du Soleil.

Their story is boldness personified.

In 1984, a group of street performers from Quebec in Canada gained funding to do a regional tour of their eclectic show – and audiences loved what they offered. Led by Guy Laliberté and Gilles Ste-Croix, Cirque du Soleil had a unique take on circus: they mixed traditional circus arts with original music and extraordinary costumes and lighting, and had no circus animals at all.

Their first tour to the United States celebrated that difference. It was titled 'We Reinvent the Circus' and it kickstarted more than 35 years of global success. By 2013, Cirque du Soleil had become a $1 billion business, with touring and resident productions in the

Americas, Asia and Europe.[4] By the start of March 2020, Cirque du Soleil was operating 44 productions around the world. Their touring shows had played to 365 million people in 1450 cities in 90 countries; in the US, Cirque du Soleil had performed 52,000 shows for more than 70 million people in Las Vegas alone.[5]

Cirque du Soleil offered stunning performances and amazing spectacle. It was also an incredibly successful business. In fact, the company was celebrated as the poster child of forward-looking corporate strategy.

One of the best-selling business books so far this century, *Blue Ocean Strategy*, highlighted Cirque du Soleil's creation and stratospheric growth as emblematic of a strategic approach they termed 'blue ocean'.[6]

The fundamental idea of blue ocean strategy is that we shouldn't limit ourselves to competing on price or quality in the same space as everyone else. Instead, our goal should be to carve out an entirely new area to operate in, where there will be no competition (at least at first) and where we can justify premium pricing.

Cirque du Soleil was a perfect example. Laliberté and Ste-Croix had flipped the circus concept on its head and reimagined the old sawdust circus rings filled with cheap seats, downtrodden animals and uneven performances. By blending elements of art, acrobatics and spectacle into a magical new experience, they had created a new and very successful entertainment niche. Cirque du Soleil was positioned as a premium product and, accordingly, justified premium pricing.

Of course, a business model based on live performances to huge audiences was not well suited to COVID-19 lockdowns. In March 2020, all 44 Cirque du Soleil productions around the world were shut down: 95 per cent of the workforce lost their jobs and the company entered bankruptcy protection in June 2020. In 2021 there was better news: with new investors on board, the company announced a staged reopening of a limited number of shows, including two in

Las Vegas in the second half of the year. However, it will be a long climb back up.

So, here's the poster child for smart strategy, lauded in books and case studies, seen in 2021 struggling back out of receivership. What do you think that tells us about their strategy? Was it wrong to start with?

No, it was incredibly successful!

Was it too dependent on one thing – revenue from live audiences? That's easier to decide in hindsight, given a one-in-a-hundred-year pandemic.

Most importantly, Cirque du Soleil's challenging journey reminds us why future planning is so difficult: it's hard to get strategy right, and it's even harder to stay right.

Strategy is key to success

The traditional definition of 'strategy' is simple: a plan to achieve long-term competitive advantage. In other words, how can you do better than your competitors, or any potential substitutes, with what you offer? And not just right now, but over time.

Your organisation's strategy is its future story:

- Who are you?
- What are you trying to achieve?
- How can you do it?
- Why is it important?

Some plans are detailed and carefully structured, documented in ring-binders and PowerPoint presentations. Other plans might be closer to scribbles on a whiteboard or a mantra that gets constantly repeated by the boss. Regardless of what they look like, **all organisations need a plan, and it's hard to get the right plan.**

Strategy is hard

There are three key reasons why strategy is hard: the world is uncertain; competition can be brutal; and strategy involves risk. Let's look at these in more detail now.

The world is uncertain

As Yoda, the master strategist and *Star Wars* character, once said: 'Difficult to see. Always in motion is the future.'[7]

We live in an uncertain world. As Cirque du Soleil's experience shows, the environment we operate in can reshape overnight. One of the leading futurists of last century, Alvin Toffler, noted that 'change is not merely necessary to life; it is life'.[8]

During the pandemic, it was tempting for many to sit back and wait for things to go 'back to normal'. But 'normal' two years ago will not be the same as normal two years from now. At the time of writing, plenty of predictions are being made about which pandemic-influenced changes are permanent (increased flexibility to work from home?) and which will be transient (Zoom drinks parties?). While the jury is still out, the one thing we can be sure about is that the post-COVID normal is not going to be the same as our pre-COVID world.

In the 21st century, digital innovation is superpowering changes in the way we work, live and govern ourselves, and in the way we plan. The power of data to inform what we do and how we plan is unprecedented, but we still don't know everything, we can't control all externalities and we can't always accurately predict the future.

Competition can be brutal

While we are aiming to do better than everyone else, so is everyone else! Often, this competition lifts everyone by raising the expectation bar. Competition can result in brilliant innovations and fantastic opportunities for consumers.

In Australia, for example, television viewers have gone from having just five metropolitan television stations to being able to choose from more than 25 free-to-air and streaming platforms, ranging from the broad (Netflix, Stan, Foxtel) to the niche (Shudder, DocPlay and iwonder).[9]

But sometimes the impact of competition is brutal.

In 2011, Australian supermarket giant Coles initiated a price war on milk, offering 1 litre of milk for $1. Other competitors, including rival supermarket Woolworths, quickly matched the offering, and the industry kept the pricing down at $1 for an extraordinary eight years.

So far, so good for consumers, but unsurprisingly, dairy farmers felt the ongoing impacts of this competition. They were forced to accept lower farm gate prices until 2019, when supermarkets raised the 1 litre price by 10 cents and promised that the increase would go directly to farmers who were struggling due to drought and low pricing.

The harsh reality of competition is that not every organisation survives. In 2015, industry analysts GDC Advisory predicted the closure of more than 6000 independent hardware retailers in Australia over ten years, thanks to the inexorable rise of 'big box' hardware retailers Bunnings and Masters.[10] The smaller stores could not compete with the large chains on pricing and range.

Ironically, the Masters chain couldn't win, either. By December 2016, its owner Woolworths had announced the closure and sell-off of all stores, after losses of more than $200 million per year. Masters had tried to do what Bunnings was already doing, and found out the hard way that competition with an established brand can end badly.

Strategy involves risk

How often do we start discussions about big issues hoping to find the answer, the solution, the absolute guarantee? Sometimes, when I'm working with an organisation, the overarching objective appears to be to find certainty – to find one decision they can make, or one action they can take, that will assure their future. How nice would that be?

But we can't always guarantee success. Sometimes circumstances change without warning. Sometimes we can't get our own act together. Sometimes history will show that we made the wrong call.

Bold strategic moves involve a decision to do things differently or a decision to do different things.

Strategic moves are predicated on research and assumptions about how others (your customers, competitors, suppliers and regulators) will respond to these moves. The more resourcing you invest in big strategic decisions, the higher the stakes. Not everything is within your control, however, so even the best-planned strategies carry some risk.

Long before COVID, Canadian strategy guru Professor Roger Martin wrote this:

> '[I]f you are entirely comfortable with your strategy,
> there's a strong chance it isn't very good… You need to be
> uncomfortable and apprehensive: True strategy is about
> placing bets and making hard choices. The objective is not to
> eliminate risk but to increase the odds of success.'[11]

Much of the strategy work I do with clients starts with acknowledging this hard truth – that we all live with some uncertainty. Our work together builds their confidence to take carefully considered steps into the unknown, rather than limiting themselves to what they know and can guarantee.

We make strategy harder for ourselves

Strategy is important, and it's hard to get right. In addition, our approach to strategy within organisations often works against the creation and implementation of bold strategy.

A few years ago, I was speaking with a group of travel industry executives about how to lead inspiring conversations when planning for the future. I asked them to think back over the past 12 months and try to remember their most exciting day at work – a day that was memorable because it made them feel inspired and energised.

It took people a while to cast their minds back, past the office Christmas party and the massive annual conference. Some settled on a day they had chalked up a big sales win, or the day they'd received a team award. When everyone had remembered what they were doing on their most exciting day at work, I asked them to raise their hand if the day they were thinking of was a strategic planning day.

Only two people in a group of 50 leaders raised their hands.

Since then, I have asked this question in multiple rooms across many different organisations, and the answers are disappointingly constant – sometimes no one puts up their hand, and at most only a few hands appear.

Why aren't people more excited about these important conversations? And why does it matter? These conversations have the potential to change the future for an organisation and its people, to unearth new insights and create new pathways. So how can they be so uninspiring?

This gap between the ideal of a strategy meeting and the reality matters, because if we're not inspired by our discussions about the future, then how can we expect people to be excited about the future we discuss? If the conversation is not engaging or surprising, then the outcomes are likely to be predictable and uninspired too.

Your strategy day should be one of the most exciting days of the year – a day that people anticipate, want to participate in and are energised to talk about afterwards.

Think about the last strategy meeting you attended and how it felt. Which end of the following spectrum was your experience closest to?

Assessing your most recent strategy meeting

←——————————————————————————————→

Time wasting	*Value adding*
Feels like another day in the office	Feels surprising and interesting
Frustration, dysfunctional behaviours	Enthusiasm, openness
No power in the room	Clear about mandate
Complex jargon	Powerful concepts
Disenfranchised	Engaged
End the session relieved it's over	*End the session excited by the future*

If you find yourself hovering to the left of this spectrum for any of these elements, then it's time to unlock more strategic power by changing your approach and your conversations.

(Not all strategy-making occurs in formal strategy meetings, of course. In Part III, I propose some better ways of approaching everyday conversations as well as your scheduled strategy meetings.)

Many of our conversations about the future fail to unlock our full strategic potential, for five main reasons:

1. We stifle imagination.
2. We don't look far enough or wide enough.
3. We don't make clear choices.
4. We set and forget.
5. We don't believe in our own power.

We stifle imagination

Why is it that so many leaders act like they're scared of imagination? The larger and more formal the meeting, the less likely you are to see leaders encouraging free-flowing creative discussions. Yet, when you're talking about the future, imagination is essential – because no one knows exactly what it will look like. We can start with information and analysis, but that's not enough on its own.

Sometimes people fall back on paint-by-numbers, highly formalised approaches because that's how they've seen it done before. You might have attended one of those sessions, in which more time is spent debating the difference between a goal and an objective than on coming up with what the goals or objectives should be. This is where 'death by framework' comes in. I regularly use great strategy frameworks, but if rigid adherence to a framework reduces or removes time for wondering aloud 'what if', then it's stifling imagination and not fostering fresh thinking.

We don't look far enough or wide enough

Eric 'Astro' Teller is the Captain of Moonshots (CEO) at X Development LLC, Google's innovation hub. X has a bold mandate. Projects at X must have the potential to solve a problem that affects millions or billions of people; they must use audacious, sci-fi technology; and they must have a chance of being achievable within the next five to ten years.[12]

With that level of ambition, the people who work at X need to be special, too. Astro Teller says, 'We seek people who are T-shaped' – meaning that they have deep expertise in one field but also bring the intellectual flexibility to collaborate across many other domains.

A willingness to be T-shaped is necessary for strategic planning. We can't be content with knowing everything about our own small world and our current operating environment. Instead, we need to be open to looking well beyond it – across sectors and time horizons. Otherwise, we run the risk of becoming too fixed in the moment, and continuing to do what we've always done.

We don't make clear choices

How many meetings have you attended that had a brainstorming session that listed multiple ideas, followed by spirited debate about the pros and cons of some options, and then... nothing? Maybe an agreement was reached to further consider all the options. Or a generic consensus statement was produced that offended no one because all the specifics had been omitted. Perhaps the meeting leaders decided to stick with status quo until more information came to light.

Making clear decisions is the boldest, most important thing we need to do in strategy. But we hesitate.

It can be difficult to get people to agree, especially when bold decisions or major changes are needed. People might be comfortable doing what they've always done and don't want to change; different points of view may produce divergent opinions; and sometimes other issues or conflicts outside the room impact on people's willingness to agree on something together.

Another key hurdle to making clear choices is our fear of failing. By choosing one path, we are taking a risk – taking one direction means we're turning away from another, and that has ramifications. The bolder the decision, the higher the stakes.

We set and forget

When I first start working with an organisation on a strategy review, I always ask the CEO or Chair to tell me about their current strategy. Sometimes, this sparks an enthusiastic summary:

> 'Our big focus is to double sales in two years' time, and the secret to our success will be broadening our customer base and re-engineering our manufacturing line to create the three new products they will need.'

Often, however, when I ask about the current strategy a leader will wave vaguely at the bookshelf. 'It's there, we'll send you a copy.' This response always makes me wonder: if people in the organisation can't immediately describe the heart of their strategy, how likely is it that they're delivering it?

The best strategy in the world has no value until it's implemented. Yet too often, the agreements we reach and the ideas we unearth go nowhere. Sometimes, the strategy doesn't get beyond the strategy meeting! People spend too little time working out how to bring it to life, or they don't actually agree with the strategy, so they conveniently overlook it. Perhaps they never understood what all the dot-points on the flipcharts meant anyway.

Even when we do get to work implementing our agreements, there's another way we reduce our strategic effectiveness – we don't continually review our progress and reassess.

Strategy is not a one-off. We can't just set and forget, because things are constantly changing inside and outside our organisations. We can't leave strategy to once-a-year meetings: instead, we need to embed strategic thinking within our organisations and our teams.

We don't believe in our own power

When I was speaking at a conference in Brisbane a few years back, I met the Chair of a large non-profit social services provider. Bob told me his organisation had recently embarked on a major strategic review process. He explained that, as one of the first steps, they had called in an expert consulting firm and asked them to present a series of future options that the Board could consider as part of their planning process.

When the time came for the consulting report to be presented, the consultants turned up not with a series of options but with one strongly recommended solution. As Bob told it, the Board was outraged and decided to shelve the report and start the strategy process again from scratch.

Now, no doubt the consultants assumed they were being helpful in providing clear advice on what they had determined to be the best way forward. But they had not taken into account the Board's commitment to be part of the process and to help design the future. The members of this Board were confident they had the ability and the power to make an impact and didn't want to give this away.

Often, however, the opposite is true. We lack confidence in our own abilities to imagine what's possible, map a path forward and make the bold strategic decisions needed to achieve success. Sometimes our leaders don't have enough trust in their people, either.

And what happens then? Sometimes nothing – we don't make the big decisions because they are too hard. Or we call in the consultants, who provide a fixed framework, hold a series of meetings and then submit a fantastic report. Once we have the report, though, what happens next? Without buy-in, even the best strategy on paper will never be brought to life, because the people needed to implement it don't understand it, don't agree with it, or don't care enough.

Can't we leave it to the experts?

At this point you might be thinking, 'If it's all so hard, why can't we leave it to the strategy experts? I don't know enough, I haven't had enough experience, I haven't been in the room for previous big decisions, I haven't made my own millions so I mustn't be strategic enough...'

I don't know if this will make you feel better or not, but the gurus don't get it right every time either!

In 2019, three titans of corporate America came together with an ambitious goal. Amazon's Jeff Bezos, Warren Buffett from Berkshire Hathaway and Jamie Dimon, CEO of JPMorgan Chase, created a joint venture called Haven Healthcare that was going to revolutionise the American healthcare system.

America has some of the best and worst healthcare in the world. The US health system costs twice as much per person as the Australian health system, but Americans have lower life expectancy.[13] Six in ten adults in the US live with a chronic disease and four in ten have two or more chronic conditions.[14] The US has an obesity rate two times higher than the OECD average.[15] Private healthcare insurance provided by employers is an important consideration in salary packages.

Haven Healthcare was established to provide better, cheaper healthcare for their combined workforce of 1.2 million employees. Warren Buffett referred to the cost of healthcare as a 'tapeworm', because of its insatiable impact on the American economy. Haven's goal was to lower the cost and improve health outcomes for their employees, and then potentially to expand the opportunity to other workers and workplaces.

The week Haven Healthcare was launched, rival health companies lost billions in value. The markets were convinced that with the weight of these proven strategists behind it, massive disruption was possible. However, in March 2021, less than three years later, the trio announced that Haven Healthcare would be disbanded.

One of the reasons cited for why they were unable to achieve their objectives was that the pandemic had increased complexity and costs for healthcare providers and patients – but there were other strategic challenges, too. Even with 1.2 million combined employees, Haven Healthcare did not have enough market power to fight the distorted incentives in the healthcare market and negotiate better deals with providers.

In addition to the external issues faced by the organisation, it was not always clear that the internal mechanisms were functioning as well as they could. Commentators questioned whether the organisation's ambitious goal had ever been translated into an implementable strategy. Another apparent issue was that the three companies were also working on their own individual healthcare initiatives, some of which could have operated in competition to Haven.[16]

After Haven Healthcare was wound down, Warren Buffett reflected, 'We were fighting a tapeworm in the American economy, and the tapeworm won'.[17]

Strategy is hard and sometimes even the best minds don't get it right, but we have more ability than we realise to identify problems and opportunities and plan a path to success.

We shouldn't underestimate our strategic power

The Australian company Stagekings designs, manufactures and installs large-scale stages and sets for major events like festivals, pop-up theatres, concerts and corporate events. Having successfully built the business over five years, founders Jeremy and Tabitha Fleming and Design & Production Director Mick Jessop were devastated in March 2020 when Australia's COVID-19 restrictions shuttered the events industry and, by extension, their business.

Jeremy explained their crisis and their determination:

'Financially the prospect was completely overwhelming, but letting all of our hard working, loyal staff go was just too much to bear. I felt sick to the core. We pretty much decided there and then that we had to – HAD to – come up with something to survive.'[18]

Stagekings became Australia's coronavirus-pivot legends. Within days, Jeremy and his team brainstormed a way to use their creative design capabilities to produce something that everyone suddenly needed – easy-to-assemble, flatpack work-from-home furniture.

Branding their range 'IsoKing', the company received 10,000 orders in the first three months, and they didn't stop there. Having succeeded with their initial bold move, the company then started building their new brand and offering. Far from losing staff, they increased their workforce from 12 to more than 50. The company has continued to expand the business, with more than 40 home products, including flatpack, easy-to-assemble bedroom and lounge-room furniture.

These bold decisions didn't start with a consultant's report or a template five-year plan. They originated from the people who know the company – its people and its potential – best.

It's hard to get right and we have to try

Planning for the future never comes with an ironclad guarantee or a promise that things will never change. That's why it's so hard, and why we hesitate to make big decisions.

It's also why we can't leave it to others. We all need to up our game when it comes to imagining and reimagining the path forward for our organisations and our businesses.

Cirque du Soleil succeeded with a groundbreaking strategy, until it was no longer fit for purpose. Haven Healthcare knew the problem but couldn't deliver a clear strategic solution. Stagekings responded creatively in a crisis and then transitioned this pivot to a longer-term growth strategy.

Strategy is not a one-off decision – it's a continually evolving conversation. That's another reason why you must involve your people in the conversations.

Over the past 25 years, I've worked with companies like Campbell Arnott's and Network Ten on public affairs strategies, organisations like Mortgage Choice and the Actuaries Institute on growth strategies, government agencies like the Department of Infrastructure on aviation and freight strategies, and many other public, private and non-profit organisations.

I've worked with smart people, enthusiastic people, burnt-out people, angry people, inspired people, people who love working together and others who can barely stand being in the same room.

I've learnt that we all have the intrinsic ability to imagine, to consider options and to map out alternative paths, but we don't always harness our collective power.

We need to be bolder

Our organisations and our communities need better solutions to intractable problems. We need innovative thinking to adapt in challenging, uncertain times. We need to develop our capacity to create and deliver more powerful strategies. We need to be bolder.

Writing about his ambitious goals for the Bill & Melinda Gates Foundation, Bill Gates stated, 'we swing for the fences'.[19] In baseball, if you 'swing for the fences', you're aiming to hit the ball well beyond the boundary. In investing, swinging for the fences means making big, bold bets on a possible winner. There aren't many bets bigger than the $50 billion invested so far by the Bill & Melinda Gates Foundation, so it's not surprising that the founders have bold ambitions.

Umit Subasi has enjoyed a stellar 30-year global career in the fast-moving consumer goods industry, in global roles with SC Johnson, Beiersdorf AG, Campbell Soup Company International and most recently as the CEO of Arnott's Biscuits. He is now a respected director, mentor and adviser on high-performance leadership.

Arnott's Biscuits is a much-loved heritage brand in Australia and beyond. While I was consulting to Arnott's, the company celebrated 150 years of operation, the 100-year anniversary of Iced VoVo and SAO biscuits, and the 50-year anniversary of the iconic Tim Tam biscuits. But no organisation can rest on its history for success. Umit describes how he worked to build a high-performance culture within Arnott's by encouraging people to think beyond boundaries and be open to learning from setbacks:

'To be able to deliver growth, risk has to be taken and failure has to be accepted. The biggest thing people are afraid of is that we will fail. And we will be labelled losers. Well, that is just wrong, because, you know, we lose only when we give up trying to win.'

Umit paints a challenging picture of what happens when we allow uncertainty and risk aversion to deter us from making bold decisions:

'[M]ost of the businesses I came across in Australia are mediocre businesses, because we operate in a risk-averse culture. Seeking to avoid failure and discouraging risk-taking just inhibits learning, and it limits growth potential.[20]

Boldness is not recklessness

Award-winning entrepreneur Glenn Keys has made plenty of big, bold strategic decisions, but notes the importance of walking a careful path when doing so:

> 'I think businesses fall into two categories. They either say, "We can't have any risk!" And so they miss a whole range of opportunities that, with some decent mitigators, would have been fantastic for their business, their shareholders and customers. The counter to that is much worse. It's the companies that go, "Risk? I laugh in the face of risk! I walked through a minefield once and I didn't explode, so I could do it every day". They think that that every day is a white swan event, not a black swan event. And so they put their shareholders, their company, their staff and their customers at risk.
>
> 'Not being at either end of the scale is really important. Being bold not reckless.'[21]

Boldness is relative

Boldness for a solo entrepreneur could be taking that first step of quitting regular, paid employment and building up a business one client at a time.

Boldness for a private-sector organisation could appear as it did in one of my earliest clients, who set out to build a global footprint from a small head office in Australia. The first strategy offsite I facilitated for them was for eight people in a small meeting room just outside Sydney. Five years later, we were flying in managers from seven countries for a global leadership strategy retreat in Abu Dhabi.

Boldness for a non-profit organisation could be taking the opportunity, while face-to-face services were suspended during lockdowns, to reimagine how those services are provided, and how they can extend their outreach in new ways.

Boldness could even be a deliberate decision to stay the course: choosing to stick to what you know you do best, despite change and uncertainty in your operating environment.

We all choose our level of ambition. But regardless of what that ambition is, we can also choose to be bolder in the way we achieve it.

If we want to be bold, we need to change our approach to strategy. We need to become more creative, more focused and more united. We can aim higher, get there faster and, most importantly, bring everyone with us on the journey. We just need to know how.

Recap

- We all know we need a plan, but creating and implementing the right strategy is easier said than done.

- The world is uncertain and we can't control everything. Competition can be brutal and can emerge from surprising places. Making strategic decisions always involves accepting some level of risk.

- To make things more challenging, all too often our approach to strategy makes success even less likely. This is because:
  - we stifle imagination
  - we don't look far enough or wide enough
  - we don't make clear choices
  - we set and forget
  - we don't believe in our own power.

- Formulaic, unimaginative approaches to strategy produce uninspired, uninspiring plans. Our fear of failure means we avoid or water down big decisions. Sometimes we have great ideas but never get around to implementing them.

- Yet we have the capability within ourselves and our organisations to become powerful strategists – to unleash more creativity, to become clearer about what's most important and to build momentum for change by reaching powerful agreements to act.

Chapter 2

The magic behind powerful strategy

In 2002, Australians Mike Cannon-Brookes and Scott Farquhar started a business creating software that would help software developers manage their workflow.

The two founders started with a business sales strategy that was unlike any other in their space. Rather than investing heavily in a dedicated sales team and chasing premium pricing, they put all their efforts into creating a remarkable product with a low entry price point to encourage direct end users to try, love and sign up to the product, and then recommend it to others.

Building on their successful model, they created a suite of products for collaboration and project management that are now used across the world by software developers, IT departments and throughout organisations.

The two founders started their business with an idea and a credit card. In 2015, the company, Atlassian, listed on the Nasdaq with a $4.3 billion market cap. It had climbed beyond $US50 billion by the end of 2020.

Atlassian's founders didn't just have a strategy – they had a strategy with powerful impact.

In 2015, Suzanne Hopman was working in social services, supporting women and children fleeing domestic violence and living in poverty. She despaired as she visited them in dingy hotel rooms, seeing them trying to create a sense of home without the essentials that we take for granted – fresh food, clothes and safety.

Suzanne used the money from selling her own home to establish the first Dignity House in the southern highlands of New South Wales. It was designed to provide a sense of home and security for women and children at the most insecure time of their lives. Dignity now provides supported crisis accommodation for men, women, children and families through 25 guest homes, offering safety, healthy food, a suitcase of new clothes and personalised support to empower people to escape homelessness. Suzanne saw the need first-hand, imagined a better way and took bold steps to make it happen. Her powerful strategy has changed countless people's lives.

So, what makes a strategy powerful? How can we create strategies that have a powerful impact in our worlds?

What is strategy?

'Strategy' is one of the most overused words in organisations. 'Corporate strategy', 'marketing strategy', 'social impact strategy', 'political strategy', 'strategic plans', 'strategic decisions', 'strategic objectives' – the list is endless. The word is used so often that people rarely stop to think about what it is (and what it isn't).

In his sweeping survey of strategy through human history, Lawrence Freedman proposes that:

> '[S]trategy remains the best word we have for expressing attempts to think about actions in advance, in the light of our goals and our capacities.'[22]

While the roots of strategy are often traced back to the earliest documented military planners, Freedman takes it back to evolution, suggesting that the political behaviour of chimpanzees in both co-operating and fighting for future benefit provide even earlier pointers to humankind's need to imagine, plan, action and adapt. (Haven't we all seen some crazy behaviours in organisations that make us wonder just how far we've evolved?)

Delve into the history of strategy and you can trace lines of thought back to ancient Greek and Roman military strategists, philosophers and poets. Strategy historians ponder the work of Chinese strategist and philosopher Sun Tzu, allude to the political musings of Niccolò Machiavelli and then focus in again on military strategy, with the likes of Prussian general Carl von Clausewitz and Swiss-French general Antoine-Henri Jomini.

The thread joining these diverse writers and thinkers is the focus on winning against an opponent. In war, this generally involved plenty of bloodshed, mostly by foot soldiers who were not privy to the strategic decisions but were still expected to turn up and play their allocated part.

Business strategy developed a life of its own in the 1960s. One thought leader was Professor Alfred Chandler, originally at Massachusetts Institute of Technology, who in 1962 provided this (non-warlike, arguably uninspiring) definition:

> 'Strategy can be defined as the determination of the basic long-term goals and objectives of an enterprise, and the adoption of courses of action and the allocation of resources necessary for carrying out these goals.'[23]

More simply put, it answers this question: What do we want to achieve over time, and how will we do it?

In the 1970s, Professor Michael Porter popularised the concept of competitive strategy: carving out a difference from competitors through 'creation of a unique and valuable position, involving a different set of activities'.[24] This focus on planning for long-term competitive advantage can be summarised in the following questions, which I mentioned in chapter 1: How can we do better than our competitors, or any potential substitutes, with what we offer? And not just right now, but over time?

In the 1980s, I suspect Henry Mintzberg shocked a few captains of industry (secretly convinced they were the modern equivalents of Alexander the Great) by likening a great strategist to a potter shaping clay. His 'emergent strategy' concept highlighted the importance of continually adapting and adjusting as situations change and opportunities are identified, rather than rigidly adhering to plans set in advance.[25] In other words, asking, 'How do we adapt and respond to the world around us in order to achieve success?'

Since then, consultants, academics and opinions about strategy have proliferated. In 2015, Boston Consulting Group consultants tracked the increase in the number of strategic planning models widely available. They clocked 81 different strategy frameworks between 1958 and 2013, and 68 per cent of these had been created in the most recent 20 years.[26] No wonder people are unsure when it comes to creating their own strategy!

In the 21st century, a new focus has emerged: strategy built on purpose.

Academics Thomas Malnight, Ivy Buche and Charles Dhanaraj researched the impact of three known drivers of high growth in companies (creating new markets, serving broader stakeholder needs and rewriting the roles of the game), and were surprised to find a fourth driver – purpose.[27] They summarised this search for purpose in the following question: What is your company's core reason for being, and where can you have a unique, positive impact on society?[28]

This commitment to purpose underpins strategy, because it's based on understanding the needs of not only the organisation but also of all the stakeholders within that organisation's ecosystem. Organisations focusing on purpose are able to build trust with their key stakeholders, reshape their value proposition and redefine their playing field.

Strategy driven by purpose is not just about an additional sponsorship deal or including corporate social responsibility (CSR) statements in an annual report. It provides opportunities for an organisation to think about their contribution to their customers, stakeholders and the wider world, and reshape their organisations around core positive ambitions.

Natalie Simmons, co-founder and Chief Operating Officer of Barefoot Citizens Consulting, works with organisations to assess the alignment between their current actions and their rhetoric (what they do versus what they say) and to craft their business strategy around purposeful outcomes. That includes establishing 'key purpose indicators' alongside key performance indicators. Simmons emphasises that 'if you become more purposeful, you see more engaged employees, customers and supply chain' – and that can lead to stronger commitments, connection and success. In other words: 'Purpose drives people, people build communities, and communities change the world.'[29]

This shift towards purpose is important, because it's changing the way people talk about strategy. Understanding purpose is essential if you're to create the shared ambition that drives the creation of powerful strategy. It can provide the momentum you need to become bolder in your own strategic planning.

So what is strategy, again?

All these descriptions of strategy include two core elements:

1. Establishing a vision of long-term success. This vision of our best possible future is powerful when it becomes a shared ambition, because then it inspires the people who will bring it to life.
2. Working out how to achieve this ambition by overcoming barriers to success and capitalising on opportunities and available capabilities. Strategic planning recognises that within every organisation there are limited resources, so prioritisation and resource allocation are central considerations. In fact, strategic decisions about resourcing and priorities are often the difference between success and failure.

Strategy is not day-to-day business planning. It's easy to swerve into this mode by getting caught up in logistics considerations, jobs lists, quarterly budgets and staffing levels. All those considerations are important, but the risk is that when our gaze drops to what's right in front of us, we stop being strategic: we forget to focus on our long game.

For our purposes in this book, let's work with a broader definition of strategy that focuses both on long-term ambitions and the pathways we can create together:

Strategy is our long game:

*   *who we are and where we're starting from*
*   *what we're trying to achieve*
*   *how we will achieve it, and*
*   *why it matters.*

The difference between good and bad strategy

Part III will focus on how to collaborate and create your own powerful strategy story. First, though, there's one more problem to consider: the fact that not all strategies are created equal. History is littered with strategies that turned out to be the wrong decisions or that failed in execution.

In the 1970s and 1980s, Kodak spent millions on developing the world's first commercially available digital camera. Kodak engineer Steve Sasson and his supervisor filed a patent for an electronic still camera in 1977, but Kodak then shelved plans for manufacturing digital cameras – it didn't want to cannibalise its existing market, selling canisters of film for non-digital devices.

Hindsight shows that was not a great strategy. Sony, Fuji and others drove the market forward while Kodak only released its first digital camera in 1993, missing its potential first-mover advantage. The company entered bankruptcy protection in 2012. In recent years it has been working to reinvent itself as a pharmaceutical components supplier,[30] but it's a long way from its heyday.

The Australian Centre for Business Growth surveyed 650 CEOs of medium and small companies about their experience with failed businesses. One quarter of the CEOs identified a lack of leadership and management (including planning) as the key reason leading to failure. By comparison, only 7 per cent of respondents identified problems with the product or service being provided, and only 13 per cent identified external factors that they were unable to mitigate.[31]

With all these challenges, and the risk of failure ever present, it is clear that we don't just need any strategy – we need the best possible strategy.

Powerful strategy

It's not enough to create our own story – we want to create a story that has impact. The focus of this book is on how we can work together to create bolder, more powerful strategies. Powerful strategy is more than a great idea – it's an idea that people commit to bringing to life.

Powerful strategy is a plan for how you can change things for the better – whether that's your customer experience, your company, your community or even the wider world. Powerful strategy is more than a great idea. It's an idea that is successfully realised: the plan is brought to life and achieves the success that you're aiming for.

So, the boldness we are seeking is not just enshrined in a strategy statement. It's encapsulated in commitment and momentum, which will drive action and bring the strategy to life.

To become powerful, your strategy needs three core elements: it needs to be a great idea, it needs a clear pathway for how to bring the great idea to life, and there needs to be a shared story. People understand and are committed to both the great idea and how to achieve it.

Let's look at each of these elements in turn.

A great idea

Think about all the classic examples of great strategy and at their core is always a brilliant idea. Steve Jobs engineered Apple's resurgence by honing in on product aesthetic and engineering for intuitive use. IKEA revolutionised home furniture by offering flatpack convenience and affordability. Stagekings identified a sudden new need for home-office furniture before people had fully appreciated the scale of Australia's COVID-19 lockdown and refocused its capabilities to deliver.

Your great idea could be a new or different:

- product line or service
- marketplace or stakeholder group
- way of engaging with your customers
- approach that distinguishes you from your competitors
- manufacturing technique
- way of delivering services
- co-operative partnership with a supplier or other stakeholder.

A great idea doesn't need to be complex. It does require fresh thinking and new perspectives.

Creative collaboration is the key to generating new ideas and planning new pathways – but creativity does not always come easily. One of the most frequent laments I hear from clients is, 'We just need some new ideas – we're not innovative enough'. In chapter 3, I show you how to foster the creative collaboration needed to generate powerful strategy, and how to overcome common innovation blocks.

A clear pathway

The second core element of powerful strategy is a clear pathway. An idea can be interesting, innovative and exciting, but it only has impact when it's brought to life.

When our two daughters were in primary school, they decided to set up a lemonade stall at the front of our house. They had the best of intentions, wanting to raise money to donate to UNICEF for children in need. They were fired up with ambition and wanted to jump into it immediately, scribbling out a poster and searching through the pantry for a lemonade bottle and plastic cups.

Now, you'd think this would be a straightforward exercise. The business model couldn't be that complicated when all the kids needed was some product to sell and people to buy it. Nonetheless, some challenges emerged. We lived in a quiet cul-de-sac, so passing trade was likely to be non-existent. No one likes unchilled, possibly flat lemonade, and an early failure with this effort could stifle their future philanthropic enthusiasm.

So, I suggested that we take a few minutes to plan how we could go about the stall to achieve the highest possible fundraising return. As we brainstormed ideas about the product and our potential customers, a bolder, better plan took shape.

The girls decided to make their own fresh lemonade and some home-baked chocolate-chip cookies to raise the quality of goods and potential revenue from the sale. We agreed to schedule the lemonade stall for a weekend day, when there would be passers-by heading to a nearby park; and they asked me to email all our local friends and invite them to visit at the designated time.

Planning the pathway gave them a better product and more customers. As a result, the girls raised more than $60 for charity (a huge success based on their ambition!) and learnt an early lesson about the value of thinking strategically.

While we're thinking about successful food-based entrepreneurs, Guzman y Gomez's founder Steven Marks opened his first Mexican fast-food store in 2006 in Newtown, Sydney, because he missed great Mexican food after moving to Australia from New York. Marks describes his vision clearly:

> 'Our vision is for GYG to be the best fast-food company in the world… We're a food company that really believes in food. We have a social and moral obligation to feed people without additives, food colouring and preservatives and that's what we're doing. We are a global game changer.'[32]

GYG has mapped out a clear pathway towards achievement of these objectives over the past 15 years, through:

- ongoing investment in researching and sourcing additive-free ingredients
- process improvements to ensure speed and quality in store
- building drive-through offerings to achieve higher turnover per store
- rapid expansion in Australia, including through franchising and global development.

Marks' bold vision of being a global game changer is coming to fruition. The company's footprint has dramatically expanded, including in the United States, and the company is now valued at $900 million. That's a lot of burritos.

Before you start googling your closest drive-in taco option, I need to pull you back to the theory behind the importance of a clear pathway.

Historian John Lewis Gaddis unpicks lessons of strategy from centuries of war, politics and literature. He underscores the importance of mapping the pathway ahead with his description of 'grand strategy':

'[T]he alignment of potentially unlimited aspirations with necessarily limited capabilities... Whatever balance you strike, there'll be a link between what's real and what's imagined: between your current location and your intended destination. You won't have a strategy until you've connected these dots – dissimilar though they are – within the situation in which you're operating.'[33]

'Connecting the dots' is a great descriptor for the pathway forward we need to create.

The history of the development of the electric car is another interesting reminder of the importance of mapping a clear pathway. In the 21st century, we're well aware of the need to reduce our reliance on traditional fuels for road transport, and over the past decade governments have started to take action to drive uptake of electric cars.

But did you know that electric cars were someone else's great idea a very long time ago? In the year 1900, 28 per cent of cars manufactured in the US were electric.[34] Over one hundred years later, in 2021, fewer than 2 per cent of new cars sold in Australia are electric.[35] So, what happened? Why aren't we all driving electric cars?

The world around electric cars changed significantly. In 1908, Henry Ford introduced the Model T Ford with its cheaper, mass-produced internal combustion engine. The development of new roads meant people wanted to drive further and faster than the electric car allowed. Petrol become cheaper and more available. Electric cars were no longer the cheapest to manufacture, they weren't as powerful and battery storage was an issue.

The result was that gas guzzlers took over the world. We now have petrol pricing and supply issues, not to mention carbon emissions challenges, and once again people are looking to electric vehicles as part of the solution.

It's a classic reminder that you need more than a great idea to create strategy with impact. A clear pathway for implementation is essential – otherwise, you end up with a very vague track petering out sooner than you think.

Chapter 4 focuses on the importance of clarity in strategic thinking. Clarity is needed at all stages of the strategy process, but particularly when mapping the path forward, overcoming hurdles and prioritising the use of scarce resources.

A shared story

The third core element of powerful strategy is a shared story. Strategy becomes powerful when it is understood, believed in and lived throughout your organisation – because then it becomes real.

Without a compelling narrative that your people can articulate, understand and, most importantly, believe in, nothing great can be achieved.

Imagine creating the best brunch in the world. Apparently, it's been achieved by an Australian-born entrepreneur in London. Prue Freeman is a former banker who established the Daisy Green Collection with her husband Tom Onions in 2012. Their Scarlett Green restaurant in Soho, London, was awarded best brunch restaurant in the world in the 2021 TripAdvisor Travellers' Choice awards.[36]

Scarlett Green is one of 11 indoor and outdoor venues across London. The Daisy Green Collection started with two vintage ice-cream vans but now is renowned for Australian-inspired, beautifully designed cafes and restaurants in buildings, canal boats and shipping containers. Daisy Green was listed in the 2018 UK Fast Track 100, ranking 52 in the list of private companies with fastest growing sales, thanks to its 66 per cent rise in sales over three years.[37]

The founders took a bold approach to growth, turning to crowdfunding through Crowdcube for their first investment round – which was massively oversubscribed and paid back early. Interestingly, many investors were also their loyal customers or became customers once they invested. Daisy Green actively celebrated that connection, using videos promoting that sense of community and shared involvement as part of the storytelling for subsequent investment rounds.

A shared story is just as important for people running their own business as it is for larger organisations and teams. I once designed a strategic planning workshop for 400 franchisees in the financial sector. Some worked in larger groups, but most were owner-operators, running their own financial advisory business under the banner of the franchise. We walked through some key steps to generating great ideas and planning pathways for achievement. Then we stopped to consider what a shared story meant for sole operators.

I encouraged them to think about others who could support them or whose understanding might help them achieve their overall objectives – for some, it was a key supplier or customer; for others it was their life partner who was sharing the highs and lows of small business along with them. It was a reminder that if you can't communicate your strategy in a way that has meaning for those you travel alongside, then chances are your strategy isn't very clear to you either.

In chapter 5, we explore how to reach the genuine consensus behind a shared story. Consensus is not about making 'lowest-common-denominator' decisions (where no one actively opposes the decision, but no one is excited about it either): rather, it's about pushing through genuine debate and discussion to inspire support and motivate action. Chapters 6 and 7 bring these concepts together by demonstrating how you can collectively embed strategic thinking and lead your organisation's strategic conversations.

Who creates powerful strategy?

When I first started developing workshops and keynote presentations on how to plan more powerfully, I spoke with a speakers' agent about the insights I wanted to offer. I was surprised to hear his perspective that 'no one is interested in talking about strategy – it's too high-end. People don't feel that's what they do unless they are in the C-suite'.

But don't we *all* do this every day? We focus on what we want to achieve and work out the best way to get there, using our abilities and available resources to overcome hurdles and increase our likelihood of success. When you think about it, every time you take an action that has any potential future impact, you're making a strategic choice.

All organisations need a strategy. Some may not be clear, some may not be smart and they may not even be documented, but all organisations are heading somewhere, whether they're clear about the destination or will be surprised by where they end up.

So, if all of us are strategists whether we like it or not, and all organisations need some kind of plan, then creating strategy is something we all need to be able to do and do well.

More than that, creating strategy together is what gives it power: because we are creating that shared story that is believed in and brought to life, and providing the momentum for boldness.

How do we unlock our own power?

Powerful strategy changes organisations, changes communities and changes lives. Strategic conversations are not just intellectual exercises – they are the keys to unlocking better ideas and creating positive impact.

We have the power within our own organisations to become bolder and more imaginative in the way we create our future. Some people sit back and assume that someone smarter must come up with the best ideas, but as my kids learnt from their lemonade stall, all of us have the potential to be strategic.

We all have the ability to imagine, create a pathway and deliver something of real value.

So, how do you create powerful strategy – how do you and your people generate the great idea, map out the clear pathway and collectively commit to a future they believe in?

If you believe the best way of creating strategy is to bring in an external adviser to write a plan for you that you can give to your people and tell them to follow, this is not the book for you. That's not to say that expert advisers aren't important and valuable partners in this process. At every step, you can greatly benefit from experts providing technical insights, different perspectives and, yes, facilitating your conversations as well.

However, the best source of powerful strategic planning is often found within organisations and committed teams. That means we need to collaborate. The secret to creating powerful strategy in uncertainty is not which framework you use. It's how you collaborate.

The importance of collaboration

We often assume that the great ideas emerge from brilliant loners working away in a lab or garage and suddenly delivering 'the answer' to an amazed world. But the best ideas come through collaboration.

American historian and journalist Walter Isaacson has written biographies of some of the most iconic individual geniuses in western civilisation, including Albert Einstein, Leonardo da Vinci and Steve Jobs. He followed those with a book called *The Innovators: How a group of hackers, geniuses and geeks created the digital revolution.*[38] This work is a fascinating walk through more than a century of genius minds and their discoveries, which catapulted us into our digital world. The most interesting part of the story is how so many of the big leaps forward needed a blend of different perspectives and skills.

This need to work together is only increasing. Isaacson predicts:

'The history of science in the 21st century will likely be dominated not by "lone geniuses"… but by collaboration and by "collective, applied imagineering".[39]

So, we need to think about how to foster creative collaborations that inspire great ideas.

Fortunately, the process of generating and discussing ideas itself generates new ideas and new combinations of possibilities. Groups of people bring different perspectives and different ways of asking questions and surfacing new options. It can be uncomfortable when divergent views are expressed and debated, but the friction generated by divergence often creates the pearls of new ideas.

Collective creation inspires commitment. Creating together not only surfaces great ideas, it inspires buy-in. No strategy is worth the paper it's written on if it's not brought to life. The more invested people are in the creation of a strategy, the more likely they are to understand it and maintain commitment to implementing it over time.

When we create strategy together, we understand and feel ownership of the story and responsibility for achieving the outcome. Often this enables us to make bolder decisions, because we've worked through the risks together and understand the decisions in the context of our full story.

The science and magic behind powerful strategy

Here's the point in the book at which you might fairly expect me to present you with a framework that you can walk through (collectively!) at your next strategy meeting. And yes, part III will provide you with some further guidance on strategy templates.

But there's one important consideration when creating powerful strategy: it's not all logic. Some magic is needed, too.

The secret to creating powerful strategy in uncertainty is not which framework you use. It's all about the quality of the collaborative process – your conversations. How you collaborate can unlock the magic behind creating powerful strategy.

For centuries, scientists, kings and, most notably, alchemists have been obsessed by the quest to find the philosopher's stone – a fabled magical substance that could transform base metals into gold and give its owner the power of eternal youth. In China, India and Ancient Greece, ancient writings document the searches and experiments done to achieve these ends. (You may even recall that J.K. Rowling's universally acclaimed book series started with boy wizard Harry Potter seeking the philosopher's stone.)

What's fascinating about alchemy is that it has always worked on two levels: pseudo-scientists' efforts to create tangible wealth (gold), along with a metaphysical search for immortality.

Much like alchemy, strategy is also a blend of the tangible and intangible. We start with information and blend this with imagination and shared ambition. This belief in our purpose gives us the strength to make choices and move ahead.

For those readers starting to shift in their seat, fearing they've just bought a self-help book hidden behind a business title, let me introduce you to Sir Isaac Newton. If you can't quite recall school history, Newton was a renowned English mathematician, physicist, astronomer and president of the Royal Society of London who made huge contributions to science and mathematics, including his three laws of motion, the concept of universal gravitation, calculus and the reflecting telescope. His *Mathematical Principles of Natural Philosophy* (the *Principia*), first published in 1687, is recognised as one of the most significant works in the history of science.

Throughout most of his life, Newton was also fascinated with the search for the philosopher's stone. Along with his respected publications like the *Principia*, he left behind reams of unpublished manuscripts, mostly written in code, about his experiments in alchemy.

Hundreds of years later, another academic, the 20th-century economist John Maynard Keynes, was so fascinated by Newton's obsession that he bought some of these manuscripts. After studying them, Keynes claimed that 'Newton was not the first of the age of reason. He was the last of the magicians'.[40]

So, here is Newton – an extraordinary scientist, so rigorous with his facts and methodologies, but also mesmerised by magical possibilities. And here is Keynes, a 20th-century economist, also fascinated with what lay behind Newton's magical thinking. Newton may have kept his scientific and magical writings separate, but I like to think that being open to other ways of seeing may have helped him apply the fresh thinking needed to achieve the breakthroughs in his academic work.

So, what is it in 21st-century strategy conversations that we need to be more open to? Strategic conversations need to be a blend of art and science, of information and imagination. We can start with what we know, but we need to also sit comfortably with uncertainty and ambiguity as part of the creative process. This is the secret to creating powerful strategy in uncertainty – but it's not for the faint-hearted. Try telling your Board that you need some more 'magic' in your strategic discussions and see how far that gets you!

Still, the reality is that we could all do with more magic moments in strategy meetings. You could also call them 'aha' moments. For example:

· when a group of people coalesce around a shared vision of success, or a new way of seeing their purpose

- when a bold idea turns into a commitment to action
- when the most important thing becomes crystal clear to every single person in the room.

I've been in the room when groups of people have those 'aha' moments, and they are magical.

Strategy alchemy happens when our conversations about the future blend many different elements together – information, imagination, purpose, the personalities in the room and the process – to ultimately create something of greater value: a powerful strategy.

We have the capacity within our organisations and with our people to unlock some magic and collectively create more powerful strategy, despite uncertainty.

We can be bolder

Dan Pink wrote:

'Greatness and nearsightedness are incompatible.
Meaningful achievement depends on lifting one's sights and pushing toward the horizon.'[41]

One of the most significant benefits I've seen from powerful strategic conversations is that they allow organisations to become bolder.

I have worked with organisations in which strategic decisions were derailed by one or more Board members who were opposed to any change at all on the grounds of 'risk'. However, when a strategic planning process enables a group to reach consensus on their ultimate objectives – their shared story – then it also provides a window for people to make braver decisions, because the risks can be viewed in the context of a wider narrative. This clarity about risk provides more freedom to consider options and opportunities before closing off ideas.

Strategic planning meetings are much more than a talkfest. They have the potential to drive meaning for your organisation, to change the way you work and even what you do, and to supercharge positive change. To do this requires a fresh approach to collaboration.

Changing the way you approach strategy:

- enables new ideas to surface
- maps a better pathway, making you more likely to succeed
- inspires people to genuinely commit to change.

If you change the way you approach your strategic conversations, you can create and implement more powerful strategy. You can go for bold.

Recap

- Powerful strategy changes organisations, changes communities and changes lives.

- Powerful strategy is built on:
  - a great idea
  - a clear pathway
  - a shared story.

- We have the power within our own organisations to become bolder and more imaginative in the way we create our future.

- To be strategic, we need to blend information and imagination with belief in our shared purpose, because that gives us the strength to make choices and move ahead.

- The secret to creating powerful strategy in uncertainty is not which framework is used, but how we collaborate.

- Changing the way we approach strategy:
  - enables new ideas to surface
  - maps a better pathway, making us more likely to succeed
  - inspires people to genuinely commit to change.

- We can make big decisions and, importantly, build momentum for positive change. We can go for bold!

PART II
THE THREE KEYS TO CREATING POWERFUL STRATEGY

IN DOUGLAS ADAMS' *The Hitchhiker's Guide to the Galaxy*, the philosopher Vroomfondel, representative of the Amalgamated Union of Philosophers, Sages, Luminaries and Other Professional Thinking Persons, sums up what we all secretly wish for:

'We demand rigidly defined areas of doubt and uncertainty!'[42]

Well-defined or not, as I've said before, the one thing we can be certain about is that uncertainty is ever-present in our life and work. Whether it's the COVID-19 pandemic, digital disruption, economic fluctuations, changing political circumstances or the kids' refusal to put on their socks, we can't control everything and we can't always predict how things will change.

At the same time, our organisations and our communities need to keep moving forward. We need innovative thinking to adapt in challenging, uncertain times. We need to find better solutions to intractable problems. We need powerful strategy.

There are three elements that fuel powerful strategic planning:

1. *Creativity.* To surface more great ideas, we need to nurture and unlock creativity.
2. *Clarity.* To map the best path forward, we need to be clear about our ultimate purpose, our options and choices.
3. *Consensus.* To bring that shared story to life, we need to reach genuine consensus.

Most organisations are good at one or two of these key elements. They may have fantastic creative thinkers, for example, but may not always be able to work through the detail needed to ensure effective implementation. Each planning session unleashes brilliant ideas, but many of them are sidelined as soon as the next great idea is put on the table. There is no follow-through and no accountability.

Another organisation may be clear on and committed to its ultimate purpose but lack new ideas or flexibility in mapping the path forward. In these organisations, the first complaint is often, 'We don't have the headspace to think about new ideas until we get extra resources'.

Other organisations may be so focused on documenting the business plan that they lose focus on what's most important, and don't always succeed in bringing their people with them on the journey. The telltale signs are that the materials prepared for their strategy session are mostly operations updates and budget forecasts, and that plenty of time is spent blaming other people or circumstances for why targets weren't met.

Strategic conversations are not just intellectual exercises – they are keys to creating living, powerful strategies that change our organisations, our communities and our lives for the better.

If you want to unlock the strategic potential of your people and your organisation, then you need to embed creativity, clarity and consensus in your strategic planning processes and in your daily conversations. In this second part of the book, we'll look at each of these core elements: what they mean, how they can help you and how you can embed them within your own strategic conversations.

Part III will go on to provide practical advice about how to blend the three elements together during discussions.

Chapter 3

Creative collaboration powers bold ideas

'To infinity, and beyond!'

Buzz Lightyear's catchcry in the movie *Toy Story* captures the extreme expectations many of us have of ourselves and our organisations when we sit down and decide to 'be creative'.

In life and work, we spend a large part of our days getting things done, ticking off tasks, producing goods or services, reporting on progress and writing lists for the next series of things we need to produce. Yet we also expect ourselves and our teams to 'think differently', innovate and 'be more creative' in the way we plan and deliver. Many strategic plans include aspirations to 'provide innovative solutions' or 'creatively solve complex problems'.

In a fast-moving, uncertain and highly competitive world, we do need to be creative and innovative when considering both the things we do and the way we do them. So, we need to get better at harnessing our collective creativity.

Think about Buzz's goal: infinity... and then beyond infinity. I'm sure a physics professor could correct me, but according to my recollection of high-school science, we can't go beyond infinity because infinity never ends. That's what makes Buzz's motto funny, and why it absolutely suits a toy who arrives in the movie with a delusional certainty that he is a Space Ranger from beyond Earth.

It reminds me of some of the meetings I've sat in where a large part of the discussion was about 'being creative' or 'being open to innovation', but often that aspiration was as creative as it got. The actual new ideas didn't quite get found. I'm not saying we're as delusional as Buzz, but we do sometimes lose ourselves in innovation rhetoric without actually producing anything new. Sometimes, too, our aspirations for creativity and innovation are set so stratospherically high that we miss the opportunity to surface fresh, smaller ideas that can then inspire more ideas.

We all have the intrinsic ability to think differently and imagine new opportunities, but these ideas don't come from another planet. The best ideas are often the ones we generate ourselves, because they are grounded in our deep knowledge of what we do and how we do it, and in genuine commitment to doing it better.

So, let's tease out how you can think differently about creativity in strategic planning, overcome barriers to innovation and fresh thinking and nurture creativity in your own conversations.

Imagination is at the core of strategy

When creating a strategy, we're designing a path to a future that doesn't yet exist – *we need to invent it*. We need to imagine what's possible and then map a path forward to achieve that ambition. Both the future we are designing and the way to get there require creative thought.

Former Chief Economist of the Bank of England Andy Haldane described this nexus:

'What set humans apart was the ability to create their imagined future. The imagined was made real. That is what is meant by creativity. Imagination *with* action is creativity.'[43]

Powerful strategy is always about more than numbers. The creativity that drives strategy does start with information (what you already know, what you can find out), but, as I've said before, this needs to be blended with imagination.

The good news is, we can be good at this!

If there's one thing the world learnt in 2020 and 2021, it was that we're more innovative and adaptable than we realised. By necessity, we began doing things differently and, in many cases, started doing different things as well. All this innovation has required creativity and ingenuity in spades.

Ferrari's prototyping team designed and built the FI5 pulmonary ventilator in five weeks in 2020. Disney ditched its reliance on big cinema movie releases to focus on direct streaming. In Australia, access to digital healthcare changed almost overnight – in February 2020 there were 20,000 virtual healthcare consultations, while over April and May there were 6 million.[44]

In the United Kingdom, Daisy Green's network of cafes and restaurants throughout London were hit hard by COVID-19 shutdowns. Wanting to engage her staff and show support for National Health Service workers, co-founder Prue Freeman was inspired to start baking. Missing Australia herself and realising that nearly 25 per cent of London's Ambulance Service were from Australia or New Zealand, Prue decided to deliver a taste of home. Working with volunteer staff at her shuttered premises, she created boxes of lamingtons to donate to hard-working paramedics and hospital staff – for every box of lamingtons bought, one box was donated to NHS workers. She called it 'Radio Lamington' and the campaign was 'Lamington for a lamington'.

The products made through Radio Lamington were anything but ordinary, with creative, whimsical lamington flavours including Passionfruit Marshmallow Pavlova, Golden Gaytime and Milo. They met a receptive audience: by September 2021, more than 50,000 lamingtons and cakes had been donated to health workers.[45]

Radio Lamington is a fabulous example of innovating in a crisis. For many organisations, innovation since the pandemic began has felt more like improvisation, because the creative thinking and adapting has all focused on short-term survival. Now the challenge is, how do we translate that adaptive creativity into our long-term visioning and planning?

Lightning versus the raindrop: creativity in strategy

Often, when I work with organisations committed to seeking out new ideas, I get the sense that everyone is waiting for lightning to strike: that they feel that if they just ask the right questions and use the right framework, a blinding flash of inspiration will hit the room and the way ahead will be clear.

Sometimes it does happen. In 2014, for example, 20-year-old friends Nic Marchesi and Lucas Patchett wanted to make a difference in the lives of people they saw living on the streets in Brisbane, Queensland. They were inspired to do something no one else had done before – provide a mobile clothes-washing service to people without a home. Their core insight was that they could fulfil a basic human need for clean clothes by providing it where people in need were, rather than expecting them to come and find it.

From their initial set-up of two washing machines and dryers in the back of a van, they built a non-profit organisation, Orange Sky, which provides mobile laundry services, showers and empathetic contact through 36 services around Australia.

Often, though, creative inspiration doesn't come like a bolt from the blue, but more like the first few drops of rain after a hot day. An idea or suggestion is dropped, a few others follow in the same spot, and suddenly you can sense a shift. Just as the first few drops of rain can herald a downpour that ultimately transforms the garden, fresh perspectives and interesting thoughts can build together to provide impetus for new ideas.

As comedian John Cleese puts it, 'By creativity, I simply mean new ways of thinking about things.'[46]

The Orange Sky founders talk about the fact that once they started out with their mobile washing service, they realised that the most valuable thing they were offering was not the clean clothes but the opportunity to sit and talk, offering friendship and support.[47] Their original inspiration – the bolt of lightning – led to something different. The growth of the service and the realisation of its potential built over time.

We need to nurture creativity

Creativity starts with being open to different ways of viewing the world, exploring opportunities and being comfortable wondering out loud.

Do you remember the five ways we make strategy harder for ourselves, covered in chapter 1? The first two are directly related to creativity:

1. We stifle imagination.
2. We don't look far enough or wide enough to spark new ideas.

Without realising it, we put up a lot of barriers to fresh thinking and fail to nurture the creativity that is essential to creating great strategy.

One of the most common questions clients ask me is, 'How do we innovate?' Often, they know they need to do things differently, to problem-solve in a new way, but they feel blocked by leaders who are risk-averse or by naysayers whose first response is to explain why something can't be done – or simply because they tell themselves, 'We're just not creative enough'.

One of the first steps to removing these blocks and nurturing creativity is to change the way we do strategy meetings. The way we design and run our strategy meetings has a huge impact on our ability to generate fresh ideas.

Formal, packed agendas with no flexibility, endless PowerPoint presentations, limited discussion time and closed rather than open-ended questions all contribute to squashing creative discussion. The more tightly you're boxed into a framework and an agenda, the more firmly the walls are locked in around you.

With Boards and senior leadership teams, another significant constraint to creative thinking is that everyone arrives at meetings intent on proving what they know and are certain of. This means that very little space is given to acknowledging what is uncertain or not yet known.

New ideas are unlikely to surface when people are bored, uninspired or too focused on what they know already.

Creative versus constructive collaboration

When my two daughters were in primary school, they loved playing in a playroom we'd set up with a little table and chairs, craft supplies, music speakers and an old whiteboard. They were still at the age of make-believe, so there were plenty of games of 'fairies' and 'families', and they loved creating those worlds in their play space. We knew things were going well when we could hear music blaring, random thumps from dancing and plenty of laughter coming from inside the room.

One day, my youngest daughter Immi was with her friend in the playroom and I realised that I couldn't hear anything – no noise, no laughter, no thumps. As any parent knows, silence can signal trouble, so I peeked in to check on them.

The scene was surprising: one serious seven-year-old was sitting at the table, while the other equally serious little girl wielded a marker pen near the whiteboard. There was a list headed 'Jobs' on the left side of the whiteboard and something that looked like a graph being drawn on the right side. I asked them what they were doing, and they promptly informed me they were playing 'meetings'. Turns out my daughter's friend's parents were both management consultants, and their kid was enthusiastic about early entry into the family business!

It's interesting that even primary-school kids had been inculcated with the sense that meetings were serious business, so they had to be serious while attending them.

Given that imagination is central to creating strategy, however, discussions about strategy should not be dull! Challenging, complex and occasionally confronting, possibly, but not boring. Your strategy meetings should be the most interesting gatherings people attend.

Creating strategy together requires collaboration, but this kind of collaboration is different to everyday constructive collaboration. Constructive collaboration is what we expect in any functional meeting. People arrive with an understanding of the purpose of the meeting, there's a clear enough process and adequate focus on the task until the job is done. I'm not saying constructive collaboration is always easy, but we at least tend to know what to expect.

Creative collaboration, by contrast, aims to inspire new perspectives and ideas. It's a more open-ended and often longer conversation – but you don't have to step too far out of your comfort zone to enable it. You simply need to embrace uncertainty, build trust and provide creative space and time.

Embracing uncertainty with curiosity

There's a myth that to be considered strategic, you need to know everything: you need to be the smartest person in the room. Now, I've worked with many Boards and executive teams over the years, and while there is one attribute that differentiates high-performing Boards from the others, it's not IQ. Nor is it net worth, or their level of commitment to a cause.

High-performing Boards walk in with curiosity. They are brave enough to say they don't know, and open-minded enough to consider other perspectives and possibilities. This gives them the power to imagine future success and alternative pathways. Strategic thinking doesn't start from certainty, it starts with curiosity.

A renowned futurist from the last century, Alvin Toffler, predicted how important it would become to be able to 'learn, unlearn and relearn':

'Tomorrow's illiterate will not be the man who can't read; he will be the man who has not learned how to learn.'[48]

So often, in strategy, we limit ourselves by collaborating with others who understand our work and bring similar perspectives, rather than challenging our thinking by actively seeking different views.

Creativity is nurtured by acknowledging that we don't have all the answers, and by allowing for the possibility of learning through failure as well as through success.

Encouraging 'not knowing' could be as simple as:

- starting a meeting by acknowledging the importance of looking beyond what we already know
- asking everyone to introduce themselves by stating one thing they're interested in learning from others in the room during the meeting
- making a list of 'known unknowns' and then predicting 'unknown unknowns' as part of your conversations about the future.

'Not knowing' can be a powerful source of inspiration and innovation, because it means we're not locked into familiar actions and pathways.

Building trust

Creativity needs trust. Trust is the foundation of psychological safety. Without it, people will never feel comfortable to be honest or explore new boundaries, and that's exactly what creative collaboration depends on.

As John Cleese memorably describes it: 'New ideas are rather like small creatures. They're easily strangled.'[49]

People will not be comfortable exploring new ideas if they feel like their contributions may be ignored or undervalued, so making it clear that all ideas will be welcomed is essential.

We all have the capacity to be strategic – we all have the ability to think through problems and create a better future for ourselves. But we sometimes underestimate the people we work with and their ability to think imaginatively, to work through a challenging change or sit comfortably with uncertainty.

Sometimes, in organisations, leaders try to shield people from difficult questions and challenging concepts. However, this instinct to restrict information or paper over uncertainties sells their teams short and makes effective planning much more difficult. I've facilitated some sessions in which I've been provided with more information about what's going to happen to the organisation in the future than the people who have been tasked with designing their future plan! That's not the way to get the most out of your people or the planning process.

Another important aspect of trust is that it works both ways – you wouldn't agree to fly with a pilot unless they were appropriately licensed and credentialled, would you? And you can't expect people to agree to big strategic leaps if they don't trust the professional expertise and genuine intent of their leaders and co-travellers.

So, you need to think about building genuine trust within your Board, or your team, well before your strategic conversations. It starts with honest, open discussions about your purpose, about the challenges you face and about the group's mandate for change.

For trust to develop, adequate time and opportunity must also be given for people to explore ideas and concepts without judgement – and this is where the next key element comes in.

Providing creative space and time

A few years ago, researchers at Mississippi State University were investigating creative problem-solving abilities. Researcher Andrew Jarosz and his colleagues asked 20 students to drink vodka cranberry cocktails until they reached the legal limit, and then tested them with word association puzzles.[50] (When I was an undergraduate student with mandatory participation in psychology research studies, we were more worried about being administered electric shocks than nursing a hangover. It's good to know some things have changed for the better in academia!)

The researchers compared the puzzle-solving efforts of the slightly drunk group with a non-drinking control group. Surprisingly, the slightly drunk group were able to solve the puzzles faster *and* with more accuracy than those who were completely sober.

I have to jump in and emphasise here that I am not suggesting hip flasks or pre-session drinks before your next strategy meeting! What I'm pointing out is that a different approach is required if you want to generate new ideas and expand your strategic mindset.

Psychologists identify the importance of daydreaming: entering a state of abstraction in which we begin to think in a different, more complex way.[51] We enter this state when we gaze up and out and let our minds wander.[52] Abstraction is the antithesis of how we're usually supposed to operate at work: we're focused on action, on productivity, on delivering. However, if we want people to think creatively, we need to enable them to feel comfortable wondering, musing out loud and not immediately knowing all the answers.

So, how do we do this? We do this by designing meetings to encourage creativity, and creating or choosing physical spaces that encourage creativity.

Meeting design

When working on draft agendas for strategic meetings, I often get pushback from leaders telling me, 'We need more presentations. We don't need that much time for discussion'. But creative synthesis takes time!

As a rule of thumb, every strategy agenda should allow at least three times more discussion time than time for presentations. I'm a big fan of requiring all factual information to be distributed in advance, so that much more of the meeting can be spent focused on future possibilities.

Creative prompts are another essential in conversations where you're seeking to inspire fresh thinking. At the end of this chapter, 'A non-creative's guide to sparking imagination' on pages 77 to 79 lists some suggested prompts, but one of the most powerful verbal prompts you can use is simply, 'What if…?'

Time is another important element. Allowing people sufficient time to wonder, to test and build ideas, is essential to enabling creativity. In this, too, participants need to commit and stay the course. All too often the most senior leaders duck out for a quick call or squeeze in an extra meeting, leaving others to continue the strategy session. These actions work against the building of creative space and trust.

Physical spaces

Creativity can be helped or hindered by the environment.

When Disney bought Pixar Animation Studios, Ed Catmull was asked to take over running Disney Animation Studios as well as Pixar. At the time, Pixar was revelling in critical and box-office successes, while Disney's animation was in a slump. Catmull was surprised to find the office space at Disney was sterile, with blank walls, empty desks and no creative prompts.[53] It sounds like many of the rooms I've seen set up for a strategy meeting.

Think about your typical meeting. You're herded into the standard boardroom that you use all the time. The information on the walls is what you see every day; everyone has their laptops open and a pile of papers in front of them, like mini barricades; and then you're expected to collaborate and do your best thinking!

Simple changes to the physical space or how you use it can make a big difference to creative conversations.

You don't have to change everything. I still work often with boardroom set-ups, because sometimes there's no other practical option (and let's face it, not everyone wants to spend all day in a beanbag!). However, think about different room set-ups or alternative venues if you can. For example, set up chairs in an open circle while the tables (and bags and devices) are moved to the side; utilise outdoor spaces for breakout discussions; or choose an interesting venue like a new gallery or an historic location, which could itself provide creative prompts.

Different perspectives are another creative prompt

In chapter 2, I mentioned the centuries-long quest of alchemy. Throughout the ages, alchemy has inspired a strange mix of mysticism, charlatanism and real science. In 1702, a brash 19-year-old German, Johann Friedrich Böttger, claimed that he had cracked the secret: he had worked out a scientific method for turning cheap metals into gold.[54]

The local ruler of Saxony, Augustus the Strong, was short of money and, hearing of Böttger, summoned him to Dresden and demanded he prove his claims. Unsurprisingly, Böttger couldn't create the promised gold. He was kept under house arrest for several years, desperately running experiments and constantly failing.

Meanwhile, Augustus the Strong still needed money and was running out of patience. And, like so many other European aristocrats at the time, he was obsessed with Chinese white porcelain. Wealthy Europeans were spending small fortunes importing teapots, plates, vases and figurines from Asia – Chinese white porcelain was considered the strongest and most beautiful, far superior to the utilitarian pottery then produced in Europe.

Another scientist was researching porcelain production and encouraged Böttger to become involved. So, the young alchemist turned his scientific attention to the mystery of porcelain, testing clays and other substances and experimenting with different firing temperatures. There was no immediate, miracle breakthrough. But more than six years after he was first placed under house arrest, Böttger discovered that a mixture including kaolin clay, alabaster and quartz, heated to at least 1300°C, produced high-quality white porcelain.

It may not have been actual gold, but it was as good as gold. In fact, European porcelain became known as 'white gold' because it brought so much wealth to its creators. Thanks to Böttger's breakthrough, Augustus the Strong established the first European porcelain manufacturing centre and made a fortune. Today his Meissen porcelain is still a renowned brand, found on the coffee tables and mantlepieces of discerning grandmothers around the world.

In this instance, the 'magic' of alchemy may not have been real, but taking a wider perspective and applying his research to a more mundane project (firing clay) became the secret to Böttger's success.

Sometimes the best place to start creative thinking is right in front of you. You can start with what you know (for example, what your best product or service is right now) and then widen your perspective. Ask, 'What value would an engineer, artist or philosopher see in this product? How would they improve it?' Or you can widen your time horizon: how might people living in 2040 deal with the problem that your product currently solves? Will the need still be there?

Restrictions can fuel creativity

The great ideas needed for powerful strategy will not emerge by doing the same things in the same way every time. You don't need endless time and money to nurture creativity, though. The most frequent concern I hear raised by organisations is this:

'We don't have time to be creative or to innovate – we're too stretched with limited budgets, time and resources.'

Think back to the cartoon stalwart Wile E. Coyote in the *Road Runner* series. In each episode, Wile E. Coyote creates a new ingenious strategy to trap and eat the Road Runner, and every time he fails. His plans and contraptions always backfire, and he ends up embarrassed and often blown up – but somehow lives on to try again.

Looney Tunes cartoonist Chuck Jones created Wile E. Coyote back in 1949. In his memoir, he outlined nine of the rules that applied to the show:

'**Rule 1.** The Road Runner cannot harm the Coyote except by going "Beep-Beep!"

Rule 2. No outside force can harm the Coyote – only his own ineptitude or the failure of the ACME products.

Rule 3. The Coyote could stop anytime – if he were not a fanatic…

Rule 4. No dialogue ever, except "Beep-Beep!"

Rule 5. The Road Runner must stay on the road – otherwise, logically, he would not be called Road Runner.

Rule 6. All action must be confined to the natural environment of the two characters – the southwest American desert.

Rule 7. All materials, tools, weapons, or mechanical conveniences must be obtained from the ACME Corporation.

Rule 8. Whenever possible, make gravity the Coyote's greatest enemy.

Rule 9. The Coyote is always more humiliated than harmed by his failures.'[55]

These are very restrictive rules! And yet despite all these restrictions, as kids we watched and rewatched the cartoon for years because the episodes all seemed uniquely hilarious.

We often believe that restrictions and limitations stop us from being creative – but as we found through 2020 and 2021, restraints can help us to think differently and be *more* creative. If we ask questions that open our minds, instead of narrowing our thinking, new possibilities emerge.

Providing people with the space and the psychological safety to wonder, to question and to not know all the answers is key to enabling the creative collaborations that produce great ideas and powerful strategy.

A story about creative collaboration

In addition to his day job at Aspen Medical, Glenn Keys established and chairs Project Independence, a non-profit organisation enabling people with intellectual disability to invest in their own home and live as independently as possible. Inspired by his son Ehren, who has Down syndrome and wanted to plan for his future home, Glenn and the Board had to design an entirely new model, he told me:

'No one has ever created a charity where people with an intellectual disability can buy their own home out of their Disability Support Pension. It's completely new. So everything we do is new. And if you want to think about it, every single decision we've made is bold, because no one's ever made it before.'

Glenn admits that while it's one thing to assess and accept risk when running your own business, the risk-assessment process with a non-profit organisation is different. With Project Independence, he says, 'we're responsible for people's lives and their future, so we have to get it right'. He explains that the process of designing the Project Independence model was highly collaborative with the Board and with interested families. This creative collaboration enabled the organisation to think differently about funding models. Rather than starting from the assumption that it was not possible to build equity using only the Disability Support Pension, Glenn and the Board took a more creative approach:

'Let's assume it is possible. Let's work back from that, and then work out what makes it possible.'

Since its establishment in 2012, Project Independence has completed two Canberra projects and is just about to start its third, providing homes and supported independent living for 30 people when the latest project is complete. The organisation is continuing to seek new opportunities to expand this unique model.

A non-creative's guide to sparking imagination

Before I summarise this chapter, I want to leave you with a handy cheat sheet on sparking imagination. Advertising gurus, artists and Booker Prize winning novelists, look away now.

You don't have to be a portfolio-carrying arts-school graduate to inspire curiosity and imagination in meetings. Here are some simple suggestions to inspire creativity.

1. **New setting, different views**

- Leave the everyday meeting room and go somewhere different. Find somewhere beautiful, or at least somewhere with windows!
- Use space differently. Do away with a boardroom table, and possibly with every table. Move between different spaces.
- If you're operating virtually, you can still change the view. Ask people to start the meeting with a backdrop chosen to highlight a key opportunity, or ask everyone to wear themed clothing; if you have budget and time, send them team sweatshirts.

2. **Play with time**

- Traditional agendas with too much detail can mean that people enter the meeting with pre-determined views about the end point ('I'll agree with item 1, oppose item 2 and am not interested in item 3 because it's only a 20-minute discussion'). If you're the facilitator of the conversation, you need a clear and very detailed plan – but participants don't need to know everything in advance. Write your agenda as a barebones outline, or even as a series of questions.
- Vary your speed. Incorporate some rapid-fire questions and answers, as well as opportunities for thoughtful reflection.

3. **Become more T-shaped**

- Invite a guest speaker with an alternative perspective to shake up the conversation before it starts.
- Provide interesting pre-reading material.

4. **Spark imagination by phrasing questions differently**

- Be more specific. For example, asking broadly 'What are your team's strengths?' often prompts a laundry list of people's ideal strengths (for example: innovative, friendly, motivated, problem-solving). A more specific question could be, 'What's one way this organisation/team is better than the last place you worked?'

- Start more questions with 'Imagine ...' or 'What if...' to allow creative thought. For example:
  - 'What if a competitor were starting up a new organisation to do our work today; how would they do it smarter?'
  - 'Imagine in three years' time this problem doesn't exist. What has changed for the better?'
- Encourage out-there thinking before you narrow things down. Include both positive and negative extremes. For example:
  - 'What would it look like if we could succeed beyond our wildest dreams?'
  - 'What are the worst things that could happen?'
  - 'If money were no object, what would we do differently?'
  - 'If we only had $10 and the contents of a fridge, how would we solve our problem?'

5. Help people let their guard down

- There is a time for responsible, rational decision-making, but it's not at the start of a strategy session. Walk the group through an opening series of visualisation discussions, without prescribed results, and you may be surprised by the ideas that can bloom during open-ended discussions.
- Ask people to draw an image (using no more than three words) of the organisation's best future and then describe what they've drawn.
- Use imagery or objects to prompt responses. Show a series of photos and ask, 'Which of these photos best reflects our organisation's current lifecycle stage and why?'

There are plenty of online resources offering more ways to inspire fresh thinking in team meetings. Try the Atlassian Team Playbook (www.atlassian.com/team-playbook), or sign up to my newsletter at www.rosieyeo.com.au/signup for regular suggestions.

Recap

- Our experiences throughout the pandemic have highlighted our capacity to be innovative and adapt in the short term. However, when it comes to strategy, we sometimes spend more time talking about the need to be innovative than coming up with new, fresh ideas.

- We can be more creative, but first we need to pull down the barriers to creativity. Providing people with the space and the psychological safety to wonder and question without knowing all the answers is key to enabling the creative collaborations that produce fresh ideas and powerful strategy.

- We can nurture creativity in our organisations by:
  - embracing uncertainty
  - building trust
  - providing creative space and time.

Chapter 4
Clarity drives bold decisions

In ancient Greece, people consulted with an oracle to seek advice from the gods before making big and small decisions. At the Temple of Apollo at Delphi, one of the most revered oracles, Pythia, was available once a month to channel divine responses to earthly questions.

The ancient historian Herodotus recounted the story of Croesus, the King of Lydia, who asked the Delphi Oracle if he should attack Persia. Her reply was: 'If you cross the river, a great empire will be destroyed'. In the time-honoured tradition of hearing what you want to hear, Croesus decided this was a great omen for success and went ahead with the invasion. History records that he did cross the river and a great empire was destroyed – unfortunately, it was Croesus' own army and ultimately his empire, destroyed by Persia.[56]

So you could call the Oracle a strategy guru (she knew the future!) or the worst strategic adviser ever (why didn't she tell it straight?). Too often in strategy we don't tell it straight. Sometimes we revert to jargon that sounds impressive but doesn't mean much. Sometimes we are swamped by too many issues and too many options. Sometimes people hear different things.

Clarity: the unsung strategy superpower

We live in a complex world. Our organisations can be complex beasts. Our customers and stakeholders are many and varied. We can access more information and complex data than ever before. On the one hand, that offers fantastic opportunities to better understand our operating environment and the forces driving change. On the other, information overload can make it harder to focus on key, relevant information.

The Cambridge English dictionary defines clarity as 'the quality of being clear and easy to understand', and 'the ability to think clearly and not be confused'.[57] In strategy, clarity sometimes goes missing.

I remember speaking with a new client about an upcoming strategy meeting. I asked her how they had fared implementing the last strategic plan, and she hesitated, then said: 'To be honest, I can't quite remember what came out of the last strategy meeting – but I'll send you the notes'.

When I received the notes, I understood why the CEO couldn't remember the outcome. The document contained a list of dot-points, presumably taken from flipchart records on the day. There were no identified themes or priorities, no timelines and no next steps. A brain dump is not a clear strategy.

Compare this to Australian bank Westpac. In May 2021, Westpac announced an ambitious plan to reduce its annualised cost base from just over $12 billion in 2020 to $8 billion in 2024. CEO Peter King had a copy of the strategic approach framed and hanging on his office wall:

'[F]ix – address outstanding issues; simplify – streamline and focus the business; and perform – sustainable long-term returns.'[58]

These words distil a major reshaping of the bank's structure and operations planned over time. Clearly a lot of thought, work and detail went into this plan, and yet it's encapsulated in three points.

Author and management consultant Chris Zook led a multi-year study identifying the root causes of long-term success for organisations, many of them very large organisations, such as Nike and IKEA. It might seem counterintuitive, but he found that one of the most significant causes of success was 'simplicity... through clarity of strategy and purpose':

'We found an increasing premium to simplicity in the world of today – not just simplicity of organization, but more fundamentally to an essential simplicity at the heart of strategy itself.'[59]

Clarity in strategy is not about retreating to insubstantial, simplified messaging, however. Productivity expert Tony Schwartz calls it 'deceptive simplicity':

'[I]deas that may seem obvious at first blush, but whose accessibility turns out to be the product of rigorous thinking, skillful synthesizing, and a commitment to clarity.'[60]

Clarity is needed throughout strategic conversations

People sometimes assume that clarity is just about messaging. Being able to effectively communicate your strategy to staff and stakeholders is very important in successful implementation, but the need for clarity runs much deeper than that.

We need to build in clarity throughout strategic planning processes in order to create powerful strategy. We need clarity of purpose, clarity about what our options are and clarity about our shared priorities. When it comes to developing strategy, clarity means knowing the stakes (purpose), delineating the options (possibilities) and focusing on what matters most (priorities).

Knowing the stakes

Suzanne Hopman is the co-founder and CEO of Dignity, a groundbreaking non-profit organisation supporting people out of homelessness. Suzanne could not be clearer about the organisation's vision: to end homelessness in Australia. She told me:

'Our mission is to empower people with dignity: to prevent, respond to, and end homelessness. So we have three quite distinct but interlinked strategies:

- In our prevention space, we look at things like our food relief programs;
- Our emergency crisis response supports someone who is homeless right now, providing supported temporary accommodation; and
- Our ending-homelessness strategy focuses on longer-term housing and wraparound supports.'[61]

These three strategies are not just documented and forgotten. Dignity has a track record of innovation and adaptability as new opportunities arise. But as Suzanne explains:

'We talk about our mission daily. For every single new idea, the very first question is, "How does that fit in either our prevent, respond or end strategies?"'

Clarity of purpose provides a clear framework for confident decision-making about new opportunities and new directions.

In 2013, Netflix CEO Reed Hastings wrote a now famous memo to investors and employees explaining the company's shift towards creating original content. It included a clear statement of intent:

'We don't and can't compete on breadth with Comcast, Sky, Amazon, Apple, Microsoft, Sony, or Google. For us to be hugely successful we have to be a focused passion brand. Starbucks, not 7-Eleven. Southwest, not United. HBO, not Dish.'[62]

Despite rapid growth and continual changes in the streaming and online entertainment world since 2013, Netflix has maintained that clarity of purpose. Their 2021 statement of their 'Long-term View' is crystal-clear, restating their strategy of being a focused passion brand:

'We don't offer pay-per-view or free ad-supported content… We are about flat-fee unlimited viewing commercial-free.

'We are not a generic "video" company that streams all types of video such as news, user-generated, live sports, porn, music video, and gaming. We are a movie and TV series entertainment network.'[63]

Powerful strategy starts from understanding your organisation's core purpose. The greater clarity you have about this, the more freedom you will have in exploring ways of achieving it.

Some of you might be thinking, 'What if we don't really know what our core purpose is? Isn't a strategic planning process all about finding that purpose?' Clarity about your purpose is essential to strategy – if you're clear at the start, that helps you plan and focus on your long game much more easily. So, if you don't have a clear sense of your core purpose, you need to at least start with a possible idea that you can hone and refine on the way through your strategy discussions. The discussion points below provide some starting questions to assess clarity about your purpose.

It's important to note that, despite the fact that we often view strategic planning as a linear process, powerful strategic discussions are not one-directional. As your conversations evolve, you will circle back to key assumptions and test these against new directions and alternative approaches.

If you're unclear about your core purpose or feel there may not be a starting agreement about what this is, spend some time working through the following three questions:

1. What does your organisation contribute to the world, your community or your customer group? What problems are you solving, or what improvements are you enabling?
2. What kind of future for your business are you and your people working towards (whether stated overtly or assumed)?
3. What are the living values of your organisation? This is not about listing statements you include in your annual report or corporate documents. Instead, take some time to think honestly about what values are seen in action in your organisation and what behaviours are rewarded. For example, are customer-service staff judged only on volume of calls or on resolution of customer issues? Does the CEO applaud lessons learnt (from unsuccessful projects) or only outright successes?

Clarity about your purpose helps you identify what the stakes are in your strategic decisions. The big decisions are those that will have the greatest impact on achieving your purpose.

Clarity of purpose directs your strategic priorities

Aspen Medical is a world-leading provider of healthcare solutions, particularly in remote and challenging areas. From its start in 2003, the company has become one of Australia's international success stories, operating across Australia, the Pacific, Africa, the Gulf region, the UK and the USA, and employing more than 4500 professionals. Whether the company is operating Ebola clinics in West Africa, managing aeromedical retrieval services for remote mine sites or designing and constructing a 51-bed COVID hospital in Australia's capital city, Canberra, within 45 days, Aspen Medical proves its mantra: 'Wherever we're needed'.

Aspen Medical was awarded 2018 Australia Exporter of the Year, co-founder Glenn Keys was recognised in 2016 as EY Entrepreneur of the Year, and the company was named as one of the best places to work in Australia on the *Australian Financial Review* Best Places to Work List 2021.

Glenn Keys has a clear vision for the company: to be the globally preferred provider of outsourced healthcare services. He is also clear about the way his organisation should operate. To that end, Aspen Medical has become one of the largest B Corps (Benefit Corporations) in Australia. Certified B Corps are 'businesses that meet the highest standards of verified social and environmental performance, public transparency and legal accountability to balance profit and purpose'.[64]

That means that the company's big strategic questions are linked not just to what they do but also to how they do it. Glenn calls it 'wisdom-based leadership': strategic decisions are based not solely on information but also on clarity about core values. He is wise about the way he prioritises strategic questions for the business. We were talking one day about this and, being ex-military, he offered this analogy:

'My view is across all the hills of Canberra, and if I look across here, there are lots of hills I could own as the high ground. But [the key is] knowing which is the right hill and saying to everybody, "Forget about all those other hills, because that hill is the most important".'[65]

When you're clear about your core purpose, then suddenly the big questions become clearer as well. Knowing what strategic questions you need to answer is essential – otherwise, you can spend a lot of time agonising over issues and debates that are not relevant to your core purpose and won't contribute to creating powerful strategy. As Glenn Keys would say, once you're clear about your purpose and the big strategic questions, though, you can 'crack on and get to the top of that hill'.

Delineating the options

So, you've clarified your core purpose, you've set your vision for future success and you've identified the big strategic questions that need to be answered. Next, you need to come up with some creative suggestions for how to achieve success, and throughout strategic discussions, you need to be clear about the options you're choosing between and the options you're saying no to. 'Delineation' is simply describing and explaining the options and their implications.

Often, when they're talking strategy, people use shorthand or jargon that sounds impressive but doesn't mean much. For example, someone might propose that as a key strategy, 'We need to better engage key stakeholders'. Fantastic! No one could argue with that… But what does it actually mean?

Delineating, or teasing out the detail behind the proposal, enables people to explore what is really meant. For example, the following questions might help clarify that 'engaging stakeholders' strategy:

1. **Who are our key stakeholders?**
- Write down the three criteria against which all stakeholders will be judged in order to determine which ones are key.
- Write down three specific examples of who these key stakeholders would be based on the agreed criteria.

2. **What does the relationship with key stakeholders look like?**

- What do these stakeholders need or want from us?
- What are we asking from each of these three stakeholders?
- What are the key messages we need to communicate?

3. **What would improved engagement look like?**

- How would we measure improvement?
- What could we do differently?
- What could we stop doing?

You can see how interrogating this simple statement ('better engage key stakeholders') will lead to more clarity on what your strategic intent should be. The strategies to support this are then likely to become much clearer, too.

This example is for just one potential strategic priority, but often when we come to these discussions, a number of options are being considered. Delineation of each option will not only help explain what we mean but also enable us to compare the options more logically. Sometimes, identifying the pros and cons of different options can help identify a new alternative that combines key benefits. Sometimes it helps people reach consensus by narrowing down points of disagreement.

Delineation helps a group make bolder decisions together, because everyone is clear about the options and the stakes. Delineation also helps with mapping a clear pathway for implementation, as people fully understand the intent behind decisions.

Focusing on what matters most

Strategy is about making choices. We choose what to do and what not to do. Sometimes we can get so involved with imagining possibilities and exploring opportunities that we forget to narrow in and focus on what matters most.

We need to move through the 'what ifs' to commit to 'what matters most'.

Clarity about what we are choosing between, and ultimately what we choose, is essential to drive powerful strategy. The client I mentioned earlier who couldn't quite remember what they last discussed in their strategy session is not a one-off case, however. When organisations get together for a strategy retreat, so much time is spent generating ideas and discussing problems that there's often not enough time spent making clear decisions.

I once facilitated a strategic planning session with SolarBuddy – a social enterprise doing amazing work to reduce the impact of energy poverty by helping kids and families gain access to light off the grid. The SolarBuddy team and their CEO Simon Doble are innovative, entrepreneurial thinkers, and it was so exciting to hear the ideas cascading right from the start of our strategy session. People were proposing new fundraising opportunities, new distribution possibilities, further expansion across the globe, and some exciting left-field ideas for building their brand and their social impact.

Their ambitions were significant and the possibilities almost endless. However, as we progressed, the team started to wonder out loud whether splitting their attention across so many brilliant ideas could potentially limit their success. As with so many non-profit organisations, SolarBuddy is powered by a small, nimble team, and their attention was being pulled in so many directions that there was a risk that projects would not be completed, or that there would not be time to think through the most effective pathways for implementing the great ideas.

The team realised they needed clarity about what mattered most.

So, we worked together with a simple assessment matrix asking two powerful questions:

1. How much would each idea contribute to reducing energy poverty?
2. How feasible was it for the organisation at this time?

Within 30 minutes, the team was able to home in on 6 immediate priorities from 20 big ideas.

The most incredible thing happened in that moment. I could feel the change in the room. It was like a weight had been lifted off people's shoulders and energy levels rose, because together they'd reached clarity about where to focus their efforts.

Complexity versus clarity during strategic conversations

Every strategic planning process demands a balancing act between deep, uncomfortable, complex thinking and the need for clarity and simplicity. I don't see this as a battle, but more a question of process. Exploratory, divergent thinking is essential to conceive and create a better future, but ultimately the outcomes of strategic conversations are only useful if they are clear and precise.

In other words: while the ideas we deal with in strategy can be complex, outputs should not be. You can't build the consensus and momentum needed to bring a shared story to life if people don't understand its core.

Strategic conversations need to widen and then focus in at different times.

I remember facilitator and consultant Dr Paul Donovan[66], years ago, drawing a series of kites on a whiteboard, which perfectly encapsulates this process. As we work through key elements of strategy, we need to widen our view (for example, with creative thinking, brainstorming and developing options) and then focus in on what's most important at that stage of the discussion (for example, with prioritising, assigning relative value and voting on preferences). This doesn't happen once but across each element of the strategic planning process.

Process clarity

I often tell people that it doesn't matter which strategy framework you use, it's the quality of the conversation that counts. Of course, some planning frameworks are better than others, depending on your organisation's circumstances, and I provide some more guidance on that in part III. But leadership of the discussion matters most.

A leader must be committed to ensuring that:

- everyone in the room understands what's being discussed
- everyone is considering the same issue at the same time
- agreements and decisions are clearly stated and clearly recorded.

Keeping people on the journey is key – which is why they need to understand and endorse the process and the end objective before you start.

There's an age-old argument about whether a tidy desk signals someone who gets things done or someone who is devoid of ideas. I have seen great ideas emerge from chaos and equally great ideas sparked from a highly structured process. In any strategic planning discussion, you'll have different types in the room with different responses to order and chaos – so you need to provide for both.

As a person who loves order and clarity, I always have a structured framework as my starting point, but I am highly attuned to when the reins need to be loosened or the process adjusted. I always have alternative approaches up my sleeve in case the conversations head in a surprising direction.

The most important thing is to ensure that your underlying process is clear, logical and flexible:

- Choose a clear process framework without complex jargon.
- Be clear about the strategic questions that need to be answered at each step of the process.
- Allow for and welcome diverse views and debate. Don't panic when disagreements arise, but explore them with curiosity.
- Delineate the options to ensure everyone understands what is being discussed and what the choices are.
- Use assessment processes to gauge support and consensus throughout the process.

Communicating with clarity about strategy

Strategy is powerful when it becomes an organisation's shared story: people understand and are committed to the great ideas and the pathways for implementation.

Clarity about what the strategy is can be blurred, however, by the jargon used to describe it. The *MIT Sloane Management Review* provides a handy Buzzword Strategy Generator[67] for those moments when you can't quite solve the problem and want to settle for a smart-sounding, yet meaningless solution.

Jokes aside, Richard Rumelt, in his great book *Good Strategy/Bad Strategy,* highlights several hallmarks of bad strategy. The first on his list is 'Fluff', which he describes as 'superficial restatement of the obvious combined with a generous sprinkling of buzzwords'. He adds:

'A hallmark of true expertise and insight is making a complex subject understandable. A hallmark of mediocrity and bad strategy is unnecessary complexity – a flurry of fluff masking an absence of substance.'[68]

After strategic decisions are made, the next step is thinking about how these should be communicated to the wider organisation. This is obviously important, but my challenge to you is this:

If you've achieved clarity throughout the process, then the communication of the strategy should be easy.

Clarity in strategy leads to clear statements about your core purpose, agreements about what matters most and commitments to act. Simple, clear agreements make for simple, clear messages to communicate. You can test the clarity of your current strategy with the Fairytale Challenge.

The Fairytale Challenge

How do you know you've achieved clarity? I've developed this Fairytale Challenge to check teams' level of consensus and clarity about future planning. All strategy is story, and of course fairytales offer an archetypal narrative, so I challenge people to describe their strategy using the following fairytale structure.

The fairytale structure aligns with a simple, traditional strategy model, where 'Vision' is your overall picture of success, 'Strengths' and 'Weaknesses' are internal factors, 'Enablers' and 'Hurdles' are the external factors that will either help you or make things more difficult, and 'Strategies' are the priority areas for action.

Try it yourself or with your team to check how clearly everyone understands and can communicate key elements of your current strategy.

A FAIRYTALE

Once upon a time, there was a (team/organisation) called

_____.

The team/organisation was _____ *(Strength)* and _____ *(Strength)*, but sometimes they could also be _____ *(Weakness)*.

The team wanted to _____ *(Vision)*.

They knew they would be helped in their quest by _____ and _____ *(Enablers)*.

But in order to achieve success, they also knew that they had to overcome some difficulties, like _____ *(Hurdles)*.

So, they decided to:

1. _____

2. _____ and

3. _____ *(Strategies)*

And they succeeded in their quest and lived happily ever after!

Clarity fuels boldness

The genuine consensus that drives implementation of strategy is only possible when people understand and support an organisation's purpose and priorities. Striving for clarity means everyone understands what's being talked about and what the ramifications are. Clarity about proposed directions is the foundation for achieving genuine consensus, which we discuss in the next chapter.

Recap

- Clarity is the unsung superhero of strategic planning.

- Clarity underpins genuine consensus because everyone understands the options. It drives implementation because the way ahead has been clearly explored. It enables bold decisions because risks can be assessed in the context of the organisation's bigger picture.

- When working on strategy, clarity means:
  - knowing the stakes (purpose)
  - delineating the options (possibilities)
  - focusing on what matters most (priorities).

- Clarity is not just about communication (although that is important).

- Clarity about your ultimate purpose opens the way to constructive, forward-focused discussion and decisions.

- A clear strategy process underpins clarity. This requires careful preparation and thoughtful leadership throughout.

Chapter 5

Consensus fuels action

Have you ever tried to negotiate with a group of friends about which restaurant to choose for dinner? Jade will suggest Indian, Dave proposes Thai and Raj reminds everyone that Jenny is allergic to spicy food. Your group ends up eating average burgers at the local pub, because it's easier than trying to navigate everyone's specific requirements at other places.

Too often, we assume that this is what consensus looks like – settling for something that will offend no one but that no one is excited about either.

The concept of consensus is much maligned. Even former British Prime Minister Margaret Thatcher once said:

> 'To me consensus seems to be... the process of abandoning all beliefs, principles, values and policies in search of something in which no-one believes, but to which no-one objects... the process of avoiding the very issues that have to be solved, merely because you cannot get agreement on the way ahead.'[69]

I'm sure we can all think of some agreements that fulfil Baroness Thatcher's criteria! Consensus is often equated with compromise.

Sometimes, people agree in the room just to finish the conversation, but then leave with no real commitment to following through. Sometimes, people are not even clear about what they've agreed to!

Powerful strategy starts with a great idea, but stalls very quickly unless two other elements are equally present: a clear pathway for implementation, and a shared commitment to both the overall goal and the path to delivery.

This is where genuine consensus comes in. Clear understanding and support are critical to creating and progressing powerful strategy. Unless consensus is reached in the room, there's a low likelihood of strategies being implemented, embedded in organisational culture or effectively communicated to other stakeholders.

Genuine consensus

Genuine consensus refers to clear agreements that are reached through open discussion and transparent assessment.

Genuine consensus is not unanimity. We don't need (and rarely achieve) 100 per cent of people in the room agreeing to everything. We do need a level of commitment to what's been agreed. As facilitator Michael Wilkinson explains:

> 'Consensus does NOT mean: "I think this is the best solution." Consensus simply means, "I can live with it and I will support it through implementation."'[70]

When I'm facilitating meetings at which key decisions are required, I often propose to participants a definition of consensus inspired by this approach: 'I can work with this and I will support it.'

Genuine consensus is grounded in shared understanding – that is, all participants understand how we arrived at this decision and what it means. Because of that understanding, they can endorse it, both during the meeting and when they're communicating the decision to others. Most importantly, they are also willing to commit to action.

The power of consensus

Building genuine consensus is essential to creating the lived, shared story that drives powerful strategy. Consensus creates commitment and momentum. When people understand and are committed to the great idea and how to bring it to life, then they will act accordingly.

Romilly Madew is the energetic CEO at Infrastructure Australia (IA), a statutory body established by the Australian Government as the nation's independent infrastructure advisor. IA provides research and advice to governments, industry and the community on infrastructure investments and reforms. Romilly joined the organisation in early 2019, and with the support of the Infrastructure Australia Board chaired by Julieanne Alroe, she has led the organisation through a quiet revolution.

There are plenty of government agencies producing useful reports, but the fearless, evidence-based advice emanating from Infrastructure Australia since 2019 has the potential to change the way governments and the private sector invest in roads, transport systems, energy, telecommunications, schools, hospitals and communities over decades to come. Infrastructure Australia has reimagined the way infrastructure proposals should be considered, by updating their assessment guidelines to include considerations of sustainability, resilience and quality of life in addition to traditional cost-benefit analysis. It has also drawn attention to the importance of engaging with local communities, including indigenous communities, as part of the infrastructure planning process.

In September 2021, the agency released its *2021 Australian Infra-structure Plan*, a 650-page, 15-year roadmap to driving economic growth across metropolitan, regional and remote Australia, and enhancing the sustainability and resilience of essential infrastructure. Julieanne Alroe's foreword highlights the plan's ambitions:

'Rather than simply projecting forward the status quo, infrastructure planning must set an ambitious vision for the country. It should anticipate and adapt to change, manage risk and deliver infrastructure that works towards – rather than against – the current and future needs of the community.'[71]

The plan highlights three key themes:

1. unlocking the potential of every place – whether cities, regional centres or remote areas
2. embedding sustainability and resilience into infrastructure decision-making
3. driving a step change in industry productivity and innovation.

While the numbers are still important (and infrastructure numbers are huge!), to me Infrastructure Australia has humanised what can be a highly technical process through their focus on these key themes.

Before taking on the CEO role at Infrastructure Australia, Romilly spent 13 years as CEO of the Green Building Council of Australia. In September 2021, she was awarded the Committee for Sydney's inaugural City Visionary award in recognition of her success in building awareness and consensus on the importance of designing for sustainability in the built environment.[72]

Romilly brought her commitment to consensus-building to Infrastructure Australia, but she would be the first to emphasise that this was not a one-woman campaign. Rather, the Infrastructure Plan and the other breakthrough initiatives by Infrastructure Australia had their genesis in ongoing strategy work with the staff and Board, as well as key stakeholders, that started in 2019:

> 'This is how we do strategy – it's consensus-driven. We
> develop it with the Board and the staff and we're very clear
> on what our purpose and our mission is… When you
> consider our Act [of Parliament] and our Statement of
> Expectations, our purpose is to provide robust, independent
> advice on infrastructure planning decision-making policy
> and priorities. And that was what we did – we went back
> to basics.'[73]

Having worked with Infrastructure Australia on Board strategy and facilitated some of their stakeholder consultations, I have seen how this focus on consensus-driven strategy permeates its strategic planning and has been a strong enabler of the robust, independent advice it is providing government, industry and the community.

Building consensus requires commitment. Romilly explains that the 2021 Infrastructure Plan was developed in close collaboration with governments, industry and communities. Infrastructure Australia's engagement program targeted more than 6500 community members and industry stakeholders across Australia's cities and regions:

> 'We didn't just sit down and come up with these big ideas…
> we captured feedback and called out what needs to be done.
> So why can we do it now? It's because we had a collaborative
> strategy. We empowered our people, we brought in
> experts. We had the Board backing because we had good
> governance.'

Infrastructure Australia's quiet revolution has only been made possible due to the level of consensus reached within the organisation and the level of genuine engagement with external stakeholders.

What happens without consensus?

What happens without consensus? Nothing! There's a classic Mark Anderson cartoon of a group of people sitting around a board table. It's the end of the meeting and the leader says:

> 'OK, now that we all agree, let's all go back to our desks and discuss why this won't work.'[74]

Genuine consensus is achieved less often than we think in strategy. As we've discussed, sometimes a lack of clarity means that people don't understand what they're supporting or agreeing to do. Sometimes a lack of effective process means that people feel disenfranchised and retreat from the open conversations needed to reach genuine shared agreements. And sometimes the leader of the group has not been clear about the group's mandate, leaving people uncertain about what they have the power to decide.

When genuine consensus is created, though, it's powerful and energising. Clear agreements give certainty and energy and ensure committed implementation. When people understand and support the pathway forward, they become effective, enthusiastic communicators to others.

Avoiding lowest-common-denominator decisions

Does the drive for consensus sometimes result in lowest-common-denominator decisions? A shared commitment to the strategy is vital to success, but when seeking consensus there's always a risk that organisations will fall back on the minimum agreements that everyone can accept, and therefore miss out on making the visionary, but more challenging, choices.

As mentioned earlier, lowest-common-denominator agreements are the decisions that no one objects to because the stakes are so low, but no one is excited about either. Genuine consensus requires being comfortable exploring and questioning divergent opinions. That requires some thoughtful process and a willingness to be curious.

That doesn't mean there won't be disagreements. In fact, if there aren't any competing or challenging views expressed during the discussion, then your strategy group is not thinking hard enough – or perhaps your brains trust is a little underfed!

Priya Parker has trained in conflict resolution and facilitated high-stakes meetings around the world. She has written about the importance of infusing every gathering with intent and meaning, and calls for a more open approach to divergent opinions:

'There is a belief, sometimes spoken, sometimes unspoken, that all meetings should be de-risked... But unhealthy peace can be as threatening to human connection as unhealthy conflict.'[75]

Jesper Sørensen and Glenn Carroll, professors at Stanford Graduate School of Business, believe that arguing is the 'best way to do strategy... provided the arguments follow established rules of engagement that are rooted in the principles of deductive logic.'[76]

Leading towards consensus

As we saw in chapter 3, leaders and facilitators play a key role in providing space and time for constructive exploration of divergent ideas without allowing the conversation to deteriorate into destructive conflict. They need to learn to sit comfortably with complexity and uncertainty during certain parts of the conversation, instead of rushing to resolution.

There are moments during some facilitation processes when I have felt lost and uncertain. Divergent views, different perspectives on what is most important, interpersonal dynamics and the awareness of the high stakes of the conversation can all combine to feel overwhelming. I've learnt, in such moments, to take a deep breath, and to *remain curious*.

Here's my other facilitation secret – the people you're working with can sometimes see the patterns and emerging views faster than you can! I've learnt to always seek guidance from the group. I ask them to survey the notes, key themes and imagery we have produced so far and consider what the pattern is that they're seeing. What are the emerging messages?

Sometimes they get there before I do. The patterns and driving forces are often clearer to people in the group because they are so attuned to the issues.

That's the challenge and the opportunity in seeking consensus – you can't force it, because the group needs to find its way together.

Of course, the conversations don't always go smoothly.

A story about trust

The shouting started 30 minutes after morning tea.

I was facilitating a Board meeting for an industry association wrestling with one significant strategic decision. The Chair and CEO had briefed me on the meeting's objective and provided the background material, including detailed analysis of all the options. While reading the materials before the meeting, the numbers told a very clear story about which was the preferred option. I went back to the Chair: 'Surely this decision is a no-brainer – why do you need me to manage a five-hour discussion about it?'

The Chair smiled ruefully. 'Wait till you meet the Board, then you'll understand.'

The session started out fine. Over coffee, the Directors chatted amicably about family, holidays and the weather – but things quickly soured as the meeting got underway.

My session plan aimed to support objective discussions about the facts and to get shared agreement on the criteria against which we could assess options for action before trying to reach a decision. I hadn't reckoned on one Board member suddenly shouting, 'There's no point in talking about the facts, because I don't believe any numbers the management puts up anyway!' The outburst prompted an eruption of views and emotions around the table.

I was seriously rethinking my career choices in that moment, but I took a deep breath and encouraged the group to acknowledge the issue, explore options for resolution and build on the Board's previously agreed definition of consensus to help them keep moving forward.

The next four hours provided my most challenging facilitation experience so far. Emotions continued to run high, but we managed to identify some of the underlying issues troubling some Directors, agree on follow-up actions to address them and reach a workable decision on the key strategic issue the meeting was called to address. The Board reached a reasonable consensus and the association went on to successfully implement its important strategic shift.

The association CEO sent me a message later that day: 'Thanks for getting us through that – at least we've given you a story to tell!'

Reaching genuine consensus requires honest discussions and active consideration of divergent views. And bold decisions are built on trust. Strategic decisions can be high stakes, and that means that people need to trust in the judgement and intent of their fellow decision-makers if they are to reach genuine consensus.

There are some Boards in which trust can be built and some in which that level of trust is never likely to be reached. I worked with one Board on which two Directors were in the middle of litigation, but their professionalism still enabled them to operate effectively during strategic discussions. I've worked with other Boards where there was a high level of dysfunction in professional relationships that reduced their ability to make bold choices. In the latter circumstances, if it's not possible to address the trust deficit directly, you may need to adjust your expectations.

Structuring conversations to build genuine consensus

Here are some keys to building genuine consensus through your next discussion:

1. Define consensus

Be clear about what you mean by consensus before you start. Consensus is not 100 per cent of people agreeing to 100 per cent of proposals but a measured decision-making process in which people agree that they are willing to work with the majority view, understand why it is the right decision at this time and commit to supporting the decision when they leave the room.

Use the definition mentioned earlier ('I can work with this and I can support this') or choose your own definition. For example, in your group you might agree that consensus is 70 per cent agreement. What's most important is that everyone understands your working definition of consensus before you start.

2. Specify the risk threshold

Clarify the organisation's risk appetite at the outset of strategy discussions. Often people's discomfort around options for change is based on their individual perceptions of risk, rather than measuring proposals against the organisation's agreed risk threshold.

3. Delineate ideas and options

Where there is disagreement, delineate different options and points of view. Find the commonalities as well as differences between options, and explore possibilities for blending or adapting options for action. Sometimes you'll find there is a lack of understanding about what the proposal is, or people are focusing on different elements at different times in the discussion.

4. Use structured processes to assess consensus

Sometimes the reason we don't walk away with genuine consensus is that we just assume the loudest voices carry the day. Ensure that everyone's opinion is sought and considered, and use structured processes to ascertain each person's views on key points – including using visual cues such as handraising, priority dots or 'five-finger' voting. This will reduce the risk of a false consensus being imposed by one or two more vocal participants.

5. Allow more space and time

Allow plenty of time and space for strategy discussions. The more innovative the idea, the more time is required to enable all decision-makers to interrogate the idea, debate options and ultimately reach effective consensus.

Start each planning process focused on delivering creativity, clarity and consensus and you'll be well on the way to helping your organisation deliver powerful strategy.

Recap

- Powerful strategy starts with a great idea but stalls very quickly unless two other elements are equally present: a clear pathway for implementation, and a shared commitment to both the overall goal and the path to delivery.

- Without consensus, strategies are unlikely to be implemented, embedded in organisational culture or effectively communicated to other stakeholders.

- Consensus is grounded in shared understanding. Participants must all understand how the group arrived at this decision and what it means. With that understanding, they can support bold decisions both during the meeting and when they are communicating the decision to others. Most importantly, they are also willing to commit to action.

- Time, space and trust are essential for building genuine consensus.

- Leaders and facilitators need to encourage the exploration of divergent ideas rather than settling for lowest-common-denominator decisions.

- Use simple tools and techniques to support the achievement of genuine consensus.

PART III
TRANSFORMING YOUR STRATEGIC CONVERSATIONS

SO, WE NOW KNOW that blending creativity, clarity and consensus can help create powerful strategies and provide the confidence to make bold decisions despite uncertainty. What does this look like in practice, though?

How can you encourage your people to become more imaginative and more open to new ideas while at the same time focusing clearly on your big objectives? How do you find the time to map out bolder future pathways while still getting your job done? How do you maintain a commitment to your agreed priorities while also being open to adapting as circumstances change?

In this part of the book, we look at how you can bring these principles to life.

In chapter 6, I show you how you can introduce more strategic thinking and a little bit more magic into your everyday work conversations, with three questions that will keep you and your people focused on your long game and inspired to continue taking big steps forward.

Chapter 7 aims to help those of you who need to run a planning process yourself, with guidance on approaches that incorporate elements of creativity, clarity and consensus. I also look at choosing a strategy framework, and when it might be better to work with a professional facilitator.

Chapter 6
Everyday alchemy
Three simple questions for powerful conversations

'Look! Here's a quokka!'

In November 2019, I travelled to Cairns to facilitate Tourism Australia's global leadership team strategy meeting. The discussions were focused on long-term strategy, but during the session, Tourism Australia's Chief Marketing Officer, Susan Coghill, gave the group a preview of Tourism Australia's Matesong campaign, which was to be launched in the United Kingdom the following month.

I came home with my ears ringing with Kylie Minogue's voice singing Eddie Perfect's genius tune. (My favourite line: 'Negotiating tricky trade deals is a shocker – but look! Here's a quokka!') I'm no advertising guru, but I was so impressed with the concept and strategy behind it, as well as the implementation program. I was sure they were onto a winner.

Just as the campaign launched in the UK, however, Australia's shocker summer kicked into gear. The effects of drought exacerbated terrible bushfires, which were closely followed by the coronavirus pandemic sweeping the world and borders slamming shut.

When crises occur, a long-term horizon very quickly contracts to dealing with immediate problems and avoiding catastrophe. In that instance, their carefully planned campaign had to be put on ice and building blocks had to be put in place for longer-term resilience and recovery. Tourism Australia quickly initiated their first ever domestically focused ad campaign, urging Australians to 'Holiday Here This Year'. Just as that campaign was kicking into gear, though, Australia's state and territory governments closed domestic borders and shut down cities, effectively telling Australians they could holiday nowhere right now. Once again, Tourism Australia had to pause the strategy and shift gears.

Heading towards the end of 2021, I was interested to ask Susan how she and her team managed to keep focused on their long game and the bigger picture throughout the year, despite constantly being side-tracked by new external crises they could not control.

Susan explained that she kept three things in focus. First, she didn't lose sight of their long game. Building international visitation is a process that can take months, if not years, as potential visitors move through the stages of awareness, consideration and then booking.

'So we understand that for us to succeed as a brand and as a destination, we always have to play the long game.'

Second, she prioritised creativity in campaign design and in crisis management.

'For us, a key principle is leveraging creativity to grow our share of voice and our share of market, using it as a true differentiator. So we have a lot of incremental conversations around the power of creativity and thinking differently, and the strategies that sit behind that as well.'

Circumstances required creative problem-solving too. The filming of Tourism Australia's 2021 national Christmas gifting campaign was completed despite domestic border closures by utilising five local film crews in different states, with virtual briefings and green rooms.

Third, she focused on their ongoing commitment to and consensus about their strategic roadmap, despite the constant need for adaptation and course corrections:

'It's essential to have a very clear sense of purpose: what you're doing and why you're doing it. One that you've clearly communicated and got buy-in for from your partners and your stakeholders.'[77]

Despite the early exit, the award-winning Matesong campaign still garnered 182 million digital impressions, 46 million online views and an estimated $40 million in earned media. It resulted in Australia becoming the number-one searched holiday destination globally.[78]

Susan is optimistic about the longer-term future for Australian tourism, too:

'We know that on the other side of the crisis, people are going to be looking for the types of holidays that we offer: our wide-open spaces, the chance to commune with nature, our wonderful wildlife, our beautiful seaside, our Indigenous experiences, our sustainable tourism experiences – these are more meaningful and have even greater value in a post-COVID world.'[79]

Everyday strategy

As I've mentioned before, strategy is never fixed, because the world we operate in is never static. Sometimes long-term planning gets parked while everyone focuses on an immediate crisis. However, as Tourism Australia has shown, we need to juggle two things: maintaining a strong commitment to our shared story and our shared future ambition, and at the same time adapting to circumstances and identifying new opportunities in a shifting landscape. The only way to do this is to ensure that the right mindset and approach is embedded in the daily life of the organisation.

That is why we can't afford to think about strategy as a once-a-year set and forget. Rather, we need to build strategic thinking into all our conversations. We need to build our strategic mindset every day, not once a year.

A few years ago, I was invited to Canberra to facilitate a strategy session for a non-profit organisation. Prior to the strategy day, I'd been briefed by the CEO and Chair and had interviewed all the directors and senior staff individually, so I had a good sense of what people wanted to talk about and the key issues to cover.

About halfway through the five-hour session, we experienced an 'aha' moment. The group was quickly reaching consensus about what was most important and how they were going to get there. One director said, 'Now I get it, it's so obvious!' By the end of the day, they had agreed on a clear direction, key strategies and the all-important first steps to start bringing them to life.

At the end of the meeting, they all said very nice things about my facilitation. But I was puzzled. Even with the most constructive, collegial, high-performing Boards, it's unusual to reach consensus on big issues so quickly. In fact, if agreement is reached too quickly you wonder whether groupthink is operating, or the focus is too narrow, or the group is being swayed by one or two dogmatic opinions.

As I thought more about it, though, I realised what had been happening. The strategy day hadn't started the discussion – it marked the high point of an ongoing conversation.

The insight I had failed to fully appreciate in my pre-session interviews was that the Board and Executive were already having thoughtful strategic conversations in every Board meeting. That's why they were able to jump to genuine consensus about their powerful strategy so quickly. (I hope I helped a bit too!) That's the power of everyday strategic conversations.

Strategic conversations change organisations

When CEOs are briefing me about the desired outcomes of an upcoming event, they'll often tell me they want their people to 'become more strategic'. I used to take this at face value, but then I started to wonder what exactly they meant. Now, I probe more deeply, and I've found that managers can mean a range of different things by 'more strategic':

- coming up with new ideas
- being more open to new ways of looking at things
- focusing on the bigger picture
- prioritising differently and avoiding being swamped by the everyday
- taking more initiative
- working smarter.

Leaders want to see their teams being active participants in the big strategy game – observing, questioning, acting and adapting to ensure the organisation stays at least one step ahead of competitors and circumstances.

Three questions that will help your people become more strategic

So, how do we help ourselves and the people in our organisations to become more strategic in the way we work and plan? How do we stay focused on winning the long game?

I've worked with many people at all levels of organisations over the past two decades, and I've noticed that some people are instinctively strategic. They scan the horizon, think laterally and imaginatively and map out several steps ahead and around. These abilities aren't confined to a certain level of education, or years of experience, or even which field people work in. Some people just seem to have an innate ability to blend information, imagination and ambition and create great strategy. Others struggle to make the connections. However, we can all learn how to become more strategic.

Umit Subasi, who I've mentioned before, has created and implemented bold, successful strategies in some tough circumstances throughout his career. He's been responsible for up to 5000 staff and $2 billion businesses. He's developed and implemented new operating models and delivered growth across Latin America, India, Africa, Europe and the Middle East. He's dealt with murky security in post-recession Russia and successfully turned around a German operation which had churned through 40 general managers in 55 years. Yet Umit confessed to me that in one of his earliest roles, he was daunted when he was invited to attend his first strategy offsite:

'That was such a steep learning curve for me as a young person in the business. Going in, I had no idea. I had seen the general manager's bullet points saying, "This is what we're going to achieve". I thought... "How are we going to do that exactly?" I just didn't know, but after those two or three days I said, "Okay, I get it now. This is how you do it, there's lots of things we can improve and build on".[80]

Taking part in those strategic planning sessions was an important learning opportunity in his early days.

Sometimes people think that strategy is something other, more senior people do in the organisation. That's not enough to fuel boldness! All of your people need to feel that they are contributing to achieving a shared ambition for your organisation. So, here are some simple ways to encourage a strategic focus within your organisation, by encouraging the following three behaviours and three repeated questions:

1. Look up and wonder, 'What if…?'
2. Look around and consider, 'What about…?'
3. Lock in and commit to 'What matters most?'

Look up and wonder, 'What if…?'

There's a school of thought in psychology focused on encouraging people to look up. When we look up and out, we enter that daydreaming state I mentioned earlier called 'abstraction', and we begin to think in a different, more complex way. Think about the last time you looked up at the stars, or out beyond the horizon. It can lead to magical moments of contemplation in which your mind expands and you feel a sense of possibility.

As we explored in chapter 3, you can't be strategic without being creative – since strategic thinking is about planning for a future that doesn't yet exist, we have to imagine what's possible. So, we need to collectively spend more time looking up. The best way to do that is spend more time together inspiring our collective imagination, by wondering, 'What if…?'

For example:

- 'What if we could expand our footprint?'
- 'What if we could communicate with our clients in an entirely new way?'
- 'What if we gave away our core product for free?'

Look around and consider, 'What about...?'

The second behaviour we should be doing more of is looking around. A strategic thinker 'looks around' – by that I mean they view situations through a wider lens. Earlier I mentioned X's focus on finding team members who were 'T-shaped': who had deep expertise but were willing and able to collaborate across a wider field. This is 'looking around'.

In my 20s, I spent a few years working as a political adviser, and I learnt very quickly the importance of understanding all points of view before a decision was made. In politics, that's mainly so you can assess the level of community and stakeholder support and opposition. In strategy, using a wider lens ensures that you identify all potential opportunities and hurdles, including those that are not immediately obvious.

Many geniuses demonstrate a commitment to 'looking around'. Leonardo da Vinci used a series of notebooks to pose a wide range of questions and his potential answers:

'Why is the sky blue? How does the heart function? What are the differences in air pressure above and beneath a bird's wing, and how might this knowledge enable man to make a flying machine? Music, military engineering, astronomy. Fossils and the doubt they cast on the Biblical story of creation.'[81]

We are so focused on our own patch of grass and on what we know best that we often forget to try and see things from other perspectives, but as strategic thinkers in organisations, we must widen our range of questions, too. It's a given that you will be asking:

- 'How are our customers' needs changing?'
- 'What are our competitors up to?'
- 'What government policy changes will impact our operations?'

The challenge is how you can broaden your questions to look beyond your immediate sphere. For example:

- 'Where are our customers looking next? What are they excited about that we don't offer?'
- 'Where are new competitors or substitutes for what we do likely to emerge?'
- 'What can we learn from other industries about new ways of operating?'
- 'What government policy changes should we be advocating for that will help us succeed over time?'

So, we look up and we wonder, 'What if...?' We look around and we consider, 'What about...?' The third behaviour that underpins bold strategic thought is to lock in and commit to what matters most.

Lock in and commit to 'What matters most?'

Strategists open their minds, consider all perspectives and *then* make decisions. This requires a laser-like focus on what's most important. The reality is that we can't do everything, so we need to choose. This is just as important in the everyday decisions as in the big strategic discussions.

You can encourage people in your own organisation to ask this question more often by:

- linking regular meeting agenda items to key elements of your strategy
- finishing each work-in-progress meeting with a summary of 'what matters most' for the week ahead
- challenging people to identify 'what matters least' on the work program (that is, what will have the smallest impact on the organisation's objectives, and whether it's really necessary).

Henry Mintzberg described strategy as being 'a pattern in a stream of decisions'.[82] Imagine a canal, with water flowing in one direction towards the ocean. The pace and flow of the water is like the momentum created when an organisation is committed to a shared ambition and united in how to achieve it. There might be some rocks below the surface that disrupt the flow, but momentum still carries the water forward. Similarly, when people in organisations have a clear sense of purpose, challenges don't throw them off course, because their shared ambition provides enough momentum.

Now imagine that same body of water with a series of openings along its flow, allowing small rivulets to branch away. You can still see most of the water flowing in the same direction, but the loss of water means that the hurdles under the surface disrupt the flow more than they used to. When organisations don't have that united commitment, momentum towards their ultimate objectives is more easily slowed or interrupted when circumstances change.

Once a commitment has been made, there will always be a series of ongoing decisions and actions that contribute to bringing the strategy to life. We tend to forget that each time we make a decision or take an action, we are effectively choosing either to stay on the path (keeping the water flowing at full momentum in the canal) or to poke holes in the canal walls.

Sometimes, of course, when the unexpected happens a significant strategic shift is needed. Much as if you were building a new canal, you need to invest time and effort in making the waterway deep and wide enough to build momentum in the new direction. Your organisation's ongoing strategic conversations are key to maintaining momentum and achieving bold ambitions.

Recap

To help reinforce the learnings in this chapter, I'll leave you to answer these questions. Try using these three questions to build the confidence in your team to make bigger, bolder strategic decisions. For the next four weeks, select one important topic to be discussed at your team meeting, and allow an additional 15 to 20 minutes to use the three-question format to encourage your team to approach the issues with a strategic mindset.

For the topic you've chosen, ask:

1. *What if?* Ask some questions that require imagination.
2. *What about?* Ask some questions that require a different perspective.
3. *What matters most?* Ask the group to prioritise one to three actions arising from the conversation. The actions should be those that will have the biggest impact on one area – whether that's sales, profits, customer loyalty or reputation. Commit to doing these first and park all other actions until the priorities are complete.

Chapter 7
Go for bold at your next strategy meeting

Imagine an organisation's typical (pre-COVID) strategy offsite meeting. Eight directors have flown in from around the country and five executives have prepared presentations and cleared their diaries for two days. Accommodation, catering for a pre-session dinner and a meeting room have been booked.

Executive time is truncated for the week before papers go out while they finalise the briefings. Things slow down at the office for the two days during the offsite, while those still at work wonder what will change. The logistics and opportunity costs are minor, however, compared with the potential value of gaining 26 days' worth of strategic insight from those 13 executive and Board brains, not to mention the exponential value obtained by blending and building on diverse ideas and perspectives.

You might not be involved in an annual strategy offsite. You might not work with a Board. However, all of us are involved in planning sessions of some kind. You might work within a small team or division; if you're running your own business, you might have a planning session on your own or with one or two trusted advisers.

Perhaps you're working with a friend on a potential new business and meeting at the pub.

One of the greatest benefits I've seen from constructive strategic conversations is that we can become bolder.

As I've discussed throughout the book, when a strategic planning process enables people to reach consensus about their shared ambitions, it also provides a window for them to make braver decisions, because the risks can be viewed in the context of what is most important. This clarity about risk provides more freedom to consider options and opportunities before closing off ideas.

In this chapter, I provide some practical advice about how to get the most from your next strategy meeting.

Finding the answer in the room

We come together in strategy meetings to celebrate what we've achieved, understand what we've learnt, inspire new ideas, challenge the status quo and commit to action. Strategic planning meetings are much more than talkfests. They have the potential to drive meaning for an organisation, to change the way we work and what we work on. They can supercharge positive change.

As leaders, we can get so caught up in the framework of strategy (Which model are we using? Are we keeping to time on the agenda?) that we fail to unlock the magic that's possible when we blend information, imagination and shared ambition during these important conversations. The goal of all strategy meetings, after all, is to 'find the answer in the room'. Participants should be empowered to assess the facts, to imagine what's possible, to reach consensus on their shared ambitions and make clear decisions about how to achieve them.

People 'in the room' (whether virtually or actually) may have a lot to lose or a lot to prove. Sometimes they bring very different assumptions, experiences and language. Sometimes their working dynamic is not conducive to building creativity and trust throughout the process. Whatever the situation, careful design, delivery and follow-through after the session can help you gain the most from your strategic planning meetings. It can help you find the answer in the room together.

How to lead strategic conversations

You've read this far in the book, so you know I believe that leaders need to expect more of – and invest more in – strategic conversations, whether they're at scheduled strategy offsites or are ongoing conversations about the future of your organisation. But sometimes it's hard to know where to start.

A strategic planning session is not your usual meeting and shouldn't feel or operate like your usual meetings. It should be considered the 'Super Bowl' of meetings. There's a lot riding on it, many people are invested in the outcome and a lot of lead-up preparation is needed. There should even be half-time entertainment, but more on that later.

Most organisations are good at setting the date, booking the venue, sending out an agenda and organising the background material. However, you need more than logistics to ensure a successful session. It needs to be designed, managed and followed through. Some leaders assume that if the agenda is confirmed and management has produced a PowerPoint deck, then the session should go fine, but 'fine' is not an adequate outcome for the investment you make in a strategic planning session.

Raising your expectations about what can be achieved from your strategic conversations is the first step towards creating more powerful strategy.

The next step in effective leadership of strategic conversations is to focus on three things:

1. *Design.* How will we structure the session? What are the key questions that need to be answered?
2. *Delivery.* How can we make the session engaging, constructive and produce results?
3. *Departure.* What feelings and commitments will people take from the session, and what happens next?

Let's look at these in more detail.

Design

You need to design your strategy discussions to help the group make decisions and reach agreements that will enable your organisation to move forward with confidence.

All too often, decisions are shelved or postponed because people call for more information, or because they question the mandate of the group to make the decision, or they can't reach agreement. When you 'find the answer in the room', it doesn't mean that you're certain of everything, because in today's world that is never possible. It means that the group has reached shared agreements about the best way forward.

You can be confident about finding the answer in the room when:

· you are clear about the big questions that need answering
· you have the right people in the room, and they have been given a clear mandate to reach agreement and move forward

- you have marshalled all necessary data and insights ahead of time
- you have a well-thought-through process that allows creative space and time
- there is a level of trust between the participants.

Plan the session carefully, then be flexible. There is a balance to be struck between sticking to a process and being open to exploring new ground. Recognise that people have different ways of approaching complex concepts.

Your structure should incorporate opportunities to be creative, clear and reach genuine consensus – this will ensure there'll be less confusion and less frustration. Incorporate some of the suggestions in chapters 3, 4 and 5 as you're planning the session. I provide more guidance about potential frameworks later in this chapter.

Delivery

My family used to own a share in a boat, and we loved spending days on the water with friends and family. Sydney Harbour is a glorious place to cruise at any time of year, but particularly in summer, when you can anchor off beautiful beaches and dive straight into the water.

I noticed a pattern to many of those days out on the boat. We would head off in the morning, excited to be out on the water and revelling in the sunshine and freedom. By the middle of the day, we had chosen a nice anchoring place, taken a swim in the harbour or ventured onshore, and then enjoyed a picnic lunch on the boat. Around the middle of the afternoon, we would start heading for home. The afternoon run was not my favourite time. The swell would pick up and clouds roll in, there was more traffic on the harbour, requiring more concentration to navigate, and the kids were salt-encrusted, tired and occasionally a little green.

I often observe a similar pattern with strategy days. We start out enthusiastic and fired up by the sense of possibility. People jump into the discussions and engage on the issues. But these are complex issues, people have diverse opinions and there are multiple factors to consider: two-thirds of the way through the meeting, people can flag and become frustrated or confused.

Often, by 4 p.m. the urgency has escalated. People rush to get through topics, throwing out or accepting ideas without careful consideration just because they've had enough of being stuck in a room. Maybe they know drinks are scheduled for 5 p.m.! At that point the risk is that you either lose people entirely or that they jump to make fast, ill-considered decisions (without genuine consensus) just to get to the end of the day and out of the room.

If you're involved in running these meetings, part of your job is tuning into the rhythms of the day and managing people's energy levels and emotions as the conversation progresses. An effective leader or facilitator will:

- *Listen.* One of the most important skills for a leader during strategy discussions is the ability to listen, not just to the person who's currently speaking, but also listening for what's unspoken or what needs to be said.
- *Be curious.* When working through complex issues and diverse opinions, as I've mentioned before, curiosity is key. If you're open to exploring new ideas and divergent opinions, you will give others in the room permission to raise and explore divergent ideas as well. Curiosity will help you sit more comfortably with the uncertainty that comes with exploring divergent views. Part of sitting comfortably with uncertainty is also accepting that no meeting will be perfect, despite all your best efforts. Powerful strategic conversations are not always easy!

- *Lighten up.* Just because the conversation is serious doesn't mean it should be dull. Strategic conversations need some light and shade, so change up the pace and approaches throughout. The half-time entertainment at the Super Bowl doesn't change the outcome of the game, but it's still part of the spectacle and fun, isn't it? In the same way, some creative, surprising moments in your strategy session can lighten the mood, lift spirits and hopefully inject some alternative thinking and goodwill into the conversations.

Remember, you need to give your people creative space, time and trust. Only then will they be able to unlock the creativity, clarity and consensus needed to generate powerful strategy.

Departure

Climbing Mount Everest is a risky proposition – and two of the most dangerous parts of the journey are at the start and near the peak. Prior to route changes made after a tragic climbing season in 2015, the Khumbu Icefall was one of the most dangerous parts of the route. Climber Jon Krakauer described each trip through the icefall as 'playing a round of Russian roulette', as sections of the huge ice pillars where the crevasses intersected could fall without warning.[83] The other very dangerous area is the 'Death Zone', above 8000 metres, close to the summit, where the air is so thin that climbers can quickly become hypoxic and delirious.

It's a dramatic comparison, but in a strategy meeting, the two most 'dangerous' points are the first and last 30 minutes. The first 30 minutes set the tone for the day and the last 30 minutes set the trajectory for the year. We all know that starting a meeting well is important, but it's easier to lose track towards the end of the day, when a certain amount of delirium has set in after too many flipcharts and many hours of debate.

Before you conclude a strategy meeting, it's essential to check for genuine consensus. Often people try to skip through this and paper over any continuing disagreements, but confirming genuine consensus is the only way to generate enough momentum to bring your bold strategies to life. Of course, it's also important to acknowledge outstanding issues and reach agreement on how these can be progressed beyond the meeting.

Documenting and sharing consensus agreements is also essential. For this, having pages of notes capturing every issue discussed is not nearly as powerful as providing a concise summary of the key agreements reached, and pointers to next steps to bring them to life.

One helpful process you can use to check understanding and commitment to the strategy is an exercise I call 'First steps'. Simply ask people to identify the first tangible action that needs to be taken to implement each of your agreements. This reinforces their understanding of those agreements and their commitment to bringing them to life. (Full implementation planning is, of course, also essential, but that's a subject for another book!)

Reaching consensus on bold strategies is a significant achievement, and it's important to finish the meeting with reflections from people in the room about what you've achieved collectively and what they are most excited about. Even just ten minutes allocated for this will end the session on a positive note.

Let's drop some assumptions about agendas and models

When a prospective client is about to start a strategic planning process with me, the first question they often ask is, 'What model will you use?' It's a valid question, because there are so many different options to choose from.

When I first started facilitating strategy with Executives and Boards, I started with a matrix that looked something like this:

A typical strategy framework

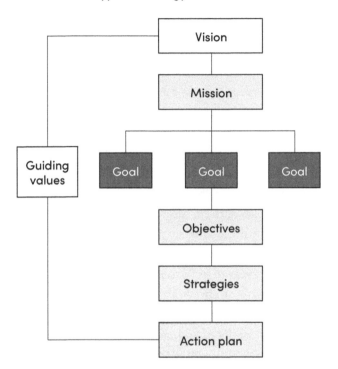

However, I quickly discovered that working with this type of structure led to continuing distractions while definitions were proposed, agreed, questioned and reclarified. You might have experienced this yourself during a strategic planning session:

- 'That's more a goal than an objective.'
- 'That strategy should be linked to a different objective.'
- 'I think the mission and vision are round the wrong way.'

The right questions are more important than the model

Models can be very useful (and later in the chapter I point you to a few models that I find useful when facilitating). However, I don't usually start with a fixed framework. Rather, I focus first on understanding what are the most important strategic questions the organisation needs to answer. Once these are clear, then I choose a framework or agenda process that will allow us to focus our time on them.

Sometimes, organisations are very clear about their core purpose but have come up against a particular strategic challenge. For example, a Board progressing in its first year of a three-year strategy may identify some key strategic issues to focus on. In other cases, it's important to go back to basics and ensure everyone is on the same page. If a Board has several new directors, for example, or major shifts have occurred for the organisation, it's important to walk through all elements of the strategic plan. This is why it's so important to be clear about the most important strategic questions before you design the agenda or choose a framework.

Meeting every year to go through the same questions using the same framework is not always a good use of time. So, before you settle on a framework, think clearly about the big strategic questions your organisation needs to address now. Some of the big strategic questions I've worked through with clients include:

- 'Do we need to redefine our core purpose? Should we even still exist?'
- 'What kind of growth are we seeking? How and where should we expand our footprint?'
- 'Who should we partner with to grow our impact?'
- 'How can we change the way we work to truly reflect our core values?'

- 'How do we reimagine how to delight our customers into the future?'
- 'How do we predict and build the capabilities that will be needed in the next 20 years in our industry?'

Selecting a framework

To reiterate: the way you talk together about strategy is more important than the framework you use. All models essentially walk you through a process of creating your long-term plan. The right models, however, do provide a logical flow and help you ask the right questions, stay on track during the discussion and reach clarity.

So, which framework or model is right for you and your organisation?

Often, the simpler the model is, the more powerful the conversation can be, because you spend more time focusing on the big issues and less time on definitions. My default position is to choose the framework that you and your team intuitively understand and can work with. I often use a five-step process, which I've incorporated in the template provided over the page. This helps people create a shared story about their long game:

- Who are we and where are we starting from?
- What are we trying to achieve?
- How will we achieve it?
- Why does it matter?

Five steps to powerful strategy

This process maps a straightforward and effective strategic planning process. You can download a free printable template of this process from my website at www.rosieyeo.com.au/resources.

Pre-session

Collate and distribute information:

- Report on progress to date mapped against current objectives.
- Environment scan: what is changing and what is staying the same in our industry for competitors, customers, suppliers, and regulatory and operating systems?
- Fresh thinking prompts:
  - One or two thought-provoking articles
  - A starter question to seek feedback from everyone at the start of the session.

1. Our starting point

Who are we?

- What is our reason for being, our core purpose?
- What have we achieved since last session?
- What have we learnt about ourselves, the way we operate and the environment we operate in?
- What should we be excited or concerned about?

2. Our shared ambitions

Set a timeframe (e.g. 1 year, 3 years, 5 years):

- What does the future look like – for our sector, for our stakeholders?
- What changes in our sector and around us are accelerating/ declining?
- If we could do anything for anyone, what could that be? How would the world be a better place as a result of our contribution?
- What is our agreed purpose for our organisation – who we are, who we serve and what difference we want to make into the future?

3. Keys to success

Connect the dots between our starting point and our future ambition:

- What needs to go right, and what will make it more difficult for us to achieve our ambition? For example, if we were mapping our progress on a board game, what would be the snakes and ladders?
- What are the factors that will have the biggest impact on us achieving our ambitions? (Select 3–5 areas of focus.)

4. Strategic priorities

For each of these 3–5 focus areas:

- What needs to change?
- What are the options for change?
- What actions are achievable and will have impact?
- For these priorities, what would be our first and next steps?

5. Commitments and reflections

Confirm consensus agreements:

- Identify outstanding issues and how they will be addressed.
- Seek individual reflections on the meeting, and the future.

Post-session

Restate the key agreements in a concise report:

- Develop an implementation plan with key tasks, timelines and responsibilities.
- Communicate your shared story.
- Establish a monitoring and review process.

There are plenty of templates and frameworks to choose from when planning a strategy session. Listed overleaf are three other strategy approaches that I find very useful.

1. Playing to Win

A.G. Lafley and Roger Martin provide a compelling framework for big-picture thinking based on five key questions in Playing to Win. Their 'strategy choice cascade' has five key questions that need to be considered together, the most important of which are 'Where to play?' and 'How to win?' Another strength of this framework is the emphasis on interrelationships between the questions. The process is not linear, as the answers to each question need to work consistently together.

2. Drivers Model

Michael Wilkinson's Drivers Model is a straightforward approach to strategic planning that can be applied to organisations of any size. The most powerful element of this model is its focus on identifying critical success factors (what needs to go right) and barriers (what could stop us) before jumping to conclusions about the best strategies.

3. Blue Ocean Strategy

This strategic lens helps organisations create new opportunities by building new market propositions. High-level creative thinking is required to define new markets and new value/cost opportunities.

For a deep-dive into other frameworks and where they are most applicable, check out the book *Your Strategy Needs a Strategy: How to choose and execute the right approach*, by Martin Reeves, Knut Haanæs and Janmejaya Sinha.

Solo business planning

Those of you working on your own may have very limited time for planning and often considerable uncertainty. My advice is, don't do it alone!

You might have some genius ideas or a new product that everyone will love. You might think you have a very clear idea of what you need to do next, or you might be very nervous about the future. I strongly recommend you talk through your strategy with at least one other trusted person. This could be your partner, a friend who understands business strategy or even a valued customer or supplier. Talking to someone else will make you put some structure behind the way you think about your strategy and ensure you're not missing any key elements.

Some emerging business owners find it very difficult to look too far ahead, particularly during times of uncertainty or when they are just too busy. If this is you, why not try working through a simplified, short-term planning exercise to clarify your thinking and build your confidence about next steps? I have a free mini-planning template designed for small business that you can download from www.rosieyeo.com.au/resources and work through with a colleague or supportive friend.

Virtual strategy sessions

Prior to 2020, I spent years insisting to all my clients that the only way to have complex, important strategic discussions was to bring everyone together in the same room.

I still believe that nothing beats the power of personal contact for high-stakes conversations. It's not just about being in the room but about the ongoing conversations that happen outside the meeting room. There's a serendipity that happens when people are clustered around a physical table or poster board, shifting and linking ideas, building on imagery, laughing out loud together. No online collaboration tool exactly replicates it.

However, there are some surprising upsides to being forced to go virtual. When a session is well facilitated, the conversation can become more democratic. The CEO is the same size as everyone else on screen. The loudest voices in the room are not always as loud when they are tiled along with everyone else, and when there are carefully structured call-outs to ensure everyone contributes. The session can become more accessible for key participants and for external advisers to provide alternative perspectives at times in the discussion, too.

There are some important things to consider with virtual strategy sessions, however. First: timing, design and preparation are different online. An eight-hour virtual meeting is not going to offer eight hours of productive engagement. Just as with other online events, agendas need to be cut and streamlined to support full participation and avoid Zoom fatigue.

For example, I transitioned a pharmaceutical company's scheduled two-day strategy offsite into a five-day online strategy sprint – the group met online for two hours every morning for five days straight. This required:

- tighter session structuring to make the most of the time available
- more background preparation and reading for participants
- an online pre-meeting, so that we could ensure everyone was comfortable with the technology and knew what was expected of them (otherwise we would have wasted the first hour of each sprint)
- follow-up with organisers after every session to reassess progress and review the next day's goals and agenda
- having thoughtful pre-session packs delivered to every participant's home, including essential background reading, morning tea treats and some tools to be used during the online session

- the use of multiple online engagement tools to support active group discussions rather than a stream of individual talking heads.

For a non-profit organisation's Board and executive strategy review, we scheduled two evening Zoom strategy sessions one week apart. Again, careful session design, a progress review between the two meetings and focused online engagement enabled the organisation to achieve their objectives for the sessions. It was even more impressive considering that one of the objectives was building rapport between new and existing Board members!

So, it is possible to do. It's not as much fun, and there is a greater challenge in building rapport, but strategy online can be done.

My expectation is that post-pandemic, organisations will still overwhelmingly recognise the benefits of coming together in person for important conversations, even more if teams are spending more time working remotely on daily tasks. Effective facilitation will be more important than ever, too, to ensure that in-person meetings offer inspiration and deliver valuable outcomes.

When to use a professional facilitator

Are you surprised it took me this long to raise this one!?

As a professional facilitator, I am proud of the work I do and the results that I enable clients to achieve. My success is not in proving how smart I am, but rather in enabling teams and Boards to surface and marvel at their own creativity, problem-solving ability and ambition for their organisation.

Reaching consensus and commitment to bold moves requires genuine buy-in from the people who must implement the decisions, however. The best facilitator in the world cannot manufacture this commitment – it comes from the people in the room.

Sometimes CEOs or Board Chairs choose to facilitate their own strategy meetings – but effective facilitation in high-stakes meetings is a full-time job. It's difficult to manage the process objectively while being a full participant in the discussions, so a CEO or Chair facilitating the strategy session loses some of their opportunity to fully collaborate. Sometimes, too, when leaders fall back into running a strategy meeting just like every other meeting they chair, they lose the opportunity to encourage people to think differently.

A professional facilitator is most beneficial in the following cases:

- The Chair or CEO wants to fully participate in the creative collaboration needed to create powerful strategy.
- There are people in the room who will process information and communicate in different ways.
- You're not confident that your team has the experience or skills to look beyond business as usual.
- There's likely to be dysfunctional behaviour and some of the heat can be taken out by using an objective, measured facilitator.

Some organisations don't have the resources to bring in an independent facilitator every time, but there may be other ways you can gain some of the benefits. Choose a simple, clear framework to help you manage the process and reduce the number of big questions you want to address. Consider whether there is another senior figure within the organisation who is not as directly involved in the issues as the CEO or Chair, and who is willing to facilitate the meeting for you.

Regardless of which approach you choose, the general principle remains the same: you should expect more of – and invest more in – your strategy meetings, because they have the potential to fuel bold decisions and to change our world.

Recap

- Raising our expectations about what can be achieved from our strategic conversations is the first step towards creating more powerful strategy.

- Leading a strategic planning session requires thoughtful design, engaged facilitation and follow-up action to bring the agreements to life beyond the meeting.

- The key elements of creativity, clarity and consensus need to be factored in as part of the design and throughout the conversation.

- The secret behind creating more powerful strategy is not which framework you use but how you manage the conversation.

- The framework or process you choose should address your most important strategic questions.

- When they are purpose-designed and well facilitated, strategy meetings are powerful sources of inspiration, innovation and commitment.

To boldly go

There's a narrow road winding around the shore of Italy's stunning Lake Como, with a driveway turning into a large stone villa that sits on a promontory jutting into the lake. In the 1950s, the property was owned by a wealthy American widow.

Just before her death in 1959, however, the Principessa Ella Walker bequeathed the villa and its beautiful gardens to The Rockefeller Foundation to become a conference centre like no other. She believed that bringing different people from different countries with different perspectives together could help solve the big problems of the world. Her goal was to provide a place that would bring together scientists, artists, policy-makers and community leaders, with the time and space for dialogue and challenging conversations. The Rockefeller Foundation gratefully accepted the endowment and opened the Bellagio Center.

In the late 1960s, there was a major food crisis in the developing world, with half of the world's population suffering from hunger and malnutrition. Populations in developing countries were growing rapidly and traditional farming systems were just not producing enough food. Major aid organisations were shipping millions of tonnes of wheat to India and other developing countries, but the problem continued to grow.

In 1967, agronomist William Paddock and his diplomat brother Paul unleashed their best-selling book *Famine 1975! America's Decision – Who will survive?*, predicting that the world was running out of food and would suffer global famine by 1975.[84] They argued that because aid-givers couldn't possibly meet the food needs of high-population countries like India, Western governments would have to choose which countries to help and which countries to abandon. In 1968, biologist Paul Ehrlich proclaimed that 'the battle to feed all of humanity is over' and predicted that hundreds of millions would die from starvation due to massive global famines.[85]

In April 1969, The Rockefeller Foundation invited 24 people to come to the Bellagio Center on Lake Como for a three-day conference on solving the global food crisis. The 24 invited guests included scientists and agricultural experts as well as public- and private-sector aid organisations. The participants arrived with the shared purpose of addressing world hunger, but with completely different ideas of how to succeed. The stakes were high; the food crisis was looming.

The aid groups and governments were focused on incremental changes to the existing approach. Their ideas were all about raising more money, faster, to increase the amount of food aid being shipped to places in need. But the scientists had a different story to tell. Scientists and agriculture experts had seen the potential for collaboration and innovation in developing countries to accelerate local food production. They wanted to show that science, not just food aid, was a sustainable solution. So, they shared examples of collaborative centres established in Mexico where the wheat yields more than tripled, and the new varieties of rice plants in southeast Asia which were called 'miracle plants' because of their higher yields and disease resistance.

Ford Foundation Program Officer for Agriculture Lowell Hardin was at the meeting and wrote about it years later. He said he knew things were on the right track when people started focusing on how, not whether, they should do this:

'By the second day, it was clear the conference was going well. People from the aid side who had just met were on first-name terms. Equally important, aid people were talking to scientists. Serious conversations continued at tea breaks on the patio, during evening cocktails and at meals. By the closing session on the third day, our thinking was converging.'[86]

Over three days of talks, the group reached some major threshold agreements:

- That the key to increasing agricultural productivity in developing countries was to apply modern scientific techniques and technologies.
- That they couldn't wait for developing countries to build up their expertise over time – they needed to immediately set up international centres of expertise in research and education as a shortcut to encouraging uptake of modern farming.
- That money should be found to fully fund the four centres of expertise and to immediately start up to 12 new centres in countries where they were most needed.

Lowell Hardin reflected later, 'It took the right mix of open-minded aid officials and dedicated scientists to achieve this, and it succeeded beyond any of our imaginings'. Three days of meetings between 24 people sharing the same purpose created the seeds of what became known as the Green Revolution – and while other issues emerged over time, this prevented a billion people in Asia and South America from starving. Instead of running out of food, India became a self-sufficient grain producer within five years.

We should never underestimate the power of bringing people together.

Sometimes strategy conversations can be difficult or contentious, and sometimes they can just be boring and unproductive.

Then there are the times, as with the conference at the Bellagio Center, when bringing people together with shared ambitions, diverse perspectives and open minds can change the world.

Every strategy session is a high-stakes conversation, in a way, because every strategy has the potential to change the world, or at least your part in it.

As leaders, we can get so caught up in the framework of strategy – which model are we using? Are we keeping to time on the agenda? – that we fail to unlock the magic that's possible when we blend information, imagination and shared ambition during these important conversations. We need to create bold, powerful strategy within our organisations, and to do that, we need to focus on imbuing strategy discussions with three key elements: creativity, clarity and consensus.

The right conversations will create strategies that become the living road map to your success – the plans that people understand and are committed to bringing to life.

We need more boldness

Our organisations and our communities need powerful strategy. We need great ideas, and clear pathways to bring the great ideas to life and build shared stories together. Living in uncertainty requires more boldness, not less.

In 2009, composer Lin-Manuel Miranda was invited to the White House to perform for then-President Barack Obama, Michelle Obama and an audience that included well-known arts luminaries. Miranda's Tony Award–winning musical *In the Heights* had opened on Broadway the previous year and Miranda was invited to perform one of the musical's hit songs as part of the Evening of Poetry, Music, and the Spoken Word.

Instead of going with the guaranteed crowd-pleaser, however, Miranda made a bold choice. With a solo piano accompanist, he performed a brand-new song called 'Alexander Hamilton' from a mixtape he'd been working on.

It's fascinating to watch the full performance on YouTube, including the audience reactions. People are intrigued with his introduction (A rap song? About a founding father?), surprised and amused by some of the verbal juxtapositions, and ultimately euphoric at experiencing this piece of creative genius. Michelle and Barack Obama led the rousing standing ovation.[87]

Lin-Manuel Miranda spent years continuing to workshop and finesse the songs of what became the global phenomenon *Hamilton: An American Musical*. But in 2009, he wasn't afraid to try out his material and to share the start of his vision – and his creative boldness transformed expectations about musical theatre.

Be proud of failure

Bessemer Venture Partners is a successful venture-capital fund which proudly lists 'The Anti-Portfolio' on their website.[88] The Anti-Portfolio is a list of the ones that got away: the investment opportunities they turned down, missing out on big returns. The names are recognisable and the stories are great fun to read. In one, partner David Cowan confesses that in 1999 and 2000, a college friend tried to introduce him to 'two really smart Stanford students writing a search engine' who were renting her garage. His reply:

'How can I get out of this house without going anywhere near your garage?'

Cowan left the house without meeting the renters – Sergey Brin and Larry Page – and missed the opportunity to get in at the ground floor with Google.

The Anti-Portfolio highlights one of the most important elements of building a high-performance organisation: that you must be prepared to fail and willing to learn from failure.

Umit Subasi believes that organisations should set themselves into a cycle:

'You set audacious goals, and then you try to reach them. You don't always reach them, but you stop, you learn, you debrief, you readjust your targets, and you go through the cycle again.'

Umit references a quote attributed to Norman Vincent Peale that he loves:

'High-performance businesses typically believe that you can take the shot at the moon. If you miss, that's okay – because you still land amongst the stars.'

We can't control everything, but we can give ourselves the best chance for success.

Living with uncertainty forces us to become more open to alternative, fresh perspectives that can lead to innovative thinking. We learn to be more confident in adapting as circumstances change. Recognising that we live in uncertain times can also make us more alert to new opportunities as well as new threats, and that can help us to become bolder.

We can develop our confidence to take bolder decisions together. It's not about knowing all the answers or taking the biggest risks.

We can give ourselves the best odds for success by focusing together on our long game:

- imagining how things could be better
- widening our perspective to plan the best path forward
- committing to what matters most.

Go on: make your next bold move.

Work with me

I am constantly inspired by people's ability to innovate, create, adapt and collaborate to change our futures. Being in the room for those 'aha' moments, when the future is clearer and brighter than anyone imagined, is one of the most fulfilling elements of my work. And I want more organisations, and more groups of people, to experience those moments.

I love working with corporate, non-profit and public-sector organisations to unlock strategic insights and create more powerful strategy.

In my strategic planning facilitation, I co-design a process matched to your circumstances and your people. My aim is not to impose solutions but to provide the creative space and prompts for your people to find the answers together.

In my keynote presentations and workshops, I inspire leaders and upcoming leaders to lead powerful strategic conversations in their own organisations.

To inquire, email hello@rosieyeo.com.au or contact me through www.rosieyeo.com.au.

Keep in touch

I would love to hear how you go introducing some magic into your strategy meetings. Please connect with me on LinkedIn (www. linkedin.com/in/rosieyeo) and share your stories and feedback.

If you want to continue the conversation, along with other like-minded leaders, please sign up to my monthly email at www. rosieyeo.com.au/signup.

In the meantime, find some creative space and time to give yourself and your team the chance to go for bold!

Acknowledgements

Writing this book about collaborative strategy would not have been possible without all my clients and friends who have invited me to be part of their most important conversations, and in the process, taught me so much.

Thank you to Glenn Keys, Romilly Madew, Susan Coghill, Suzanne Hopman, Natalie Simmons and Umit Subasi for your generosity in sharing your experiences and insights for this book.

To Lesley Williams, editor Vanessa Smith, Eleanor Reader and Will Allen at Major Street Publishing: my heartfelt gratitude for your professionalism and your encouragement along the way.

Thank you also to:

Kelly Irving, Zara and Troy Love for teaching me about powerful communication in all its forms.

Sophie Scott and Fiona Robertson for sharing your experiences of the writing journey.

Tricia Weekes for asking all the right questions for the past 30 years.

Andrea and Peter Werner for always being around the corner.

Angela, Emma and Megan for keeping me outdoors when I should have been writing.

Mum, Dad, and my extended family for love, laughter and loudness.

Special thanks to the three people who are with me every step of the way in life and work: my husband Ian Kirkham and our daughters Lily and Imogen.

About the author
Rosie Yeo MBA (Exec), BA (Hons), GAICD

Rosie is the go-to strategist for boards, executive teams and business leaders because of her skill in helping people collectively imagine and achieve a better future.

Drawing on her decades of experience and comprehensive knowledge of strategic theory, Rosie offers a fresh, engaging take on future planning that cuts through the jargon to provide practical advice and inspiration.

Rosie's experience as a public affairs strategist, Board director and corporate adviser provides unique insights into how organisations design and implement their big plans. She has worked with corporate, government and non-profit organisations in healthcare, financial services, infrastructure, tourism, FMCG and media.

Rosie lives in Sydney, Australia, and works across the Asia-Pacific region with Boards, executive teams and stakeholders to steer complex discussions, design better futures and deliver positive change. In her keynote speeches and workshops Rosie inspires us all to become more powerful strategists in our life and work.

References

1   S. Morrison (Prime Minister of Australia) & G. Hunt
    (Minister for Health), *$2 billion to extend critical health
    services across Australia*, media release, Parliament House,
    Canberra, 18 September 2020, https://www.pm.gov.au/
    media/2-billion-extend-critical-health-services-across-australia.

2   J. Allen, 'A new social contract: planning in a post-Covid-19 world',
    Founder's Mentality Blog, Bain & Company, 25 May 2020, https://
    www.bain.com/insights/a-new-social-contract-planning-post-
    covid-19-world-fm-blog/.

3   Australian Securities & Investments Commission (ASIC),
    Australian insolvency statistics, November 2021, https://
    asic.gov.au/regulatory-resources/find-a-document/statistics/
    insolvency-statistics/insolvency-statistics-series-1-companies-
    entering-external-administration-and-controller-appointments/.

4   K. Gittleson, 'How Cirque du Soleil became a billion dollar
    business', BBC News, 12 December 2013, www.bbc.com/news/
    business-25311503.

5   TV News Desk, 'MGM will release documentary on the resurgence
    of Cirque du Soleil', *Broadway World*, 30 June 2021, https://www.
    broadwayworld.com/las-vegas/article/MGM-Will-Produce-
    Exclusive-Documentary-on-Cirque-du-Soleil-20210630.

6   W.C. Kim & R.A. Mauborgne, *Blue Ocean Strategy: How to create
    uncontested market space and make the competition irrelevant*,
    Harvard Business Review Press, Boston, Massachusetts, 2015.

7   I. Kershner (director), *Star Wars: The Empire Strikes Back (Episode 5)*, Lucasfilm Ltd, San Francisco, 1980.

8   A. Toffler, *Future Shock*, Pan Books, London, 1970.

9   D. Heckscher, 'What streaming services are there in Australia?', Canstarblue.com.au, 9 October 2021, www.canstarblue.com.au/streaming/australia-streaming-services/.

10 A. Sadauskas, 'Over 6000 independent hardware stores to close as Bunnings and Masters nail the competition', *SmartCompany*, 15 April 2015, https://www.smartcompany.com.au/growth/over-6000-independent-hardware-stores-to-close-as-bunnings-and-masters-nail-the-competition/.

11 R.L. Martin, 'The big lie of strategic planning', *Harvard Business Review*, January–February 2014.

12 Astro Teller, 'A peek inside the moonshot factory operating manual', X.company, 24 July 2016, https://blog.x.company/a-peek-inside-the-moonshot-factory-operating-manual-f5c33c9ab4d7.

13 A. Duckett, 'More expensive but less effective: the US healthcare system explained', *The Conversation*, 19 November 2020.

14 National Center for Chronic Disease Prevention and Health Promotion, 'Chronic Diseases in America', CDC.gov, www.cdc.gov/chronicdisease/resources/infographic/chronic-diseases.htm.

15 R. Tikkanen & M.K. Abrams, 'U.S. health care from a global perspective, 2019: Higher spending, worse outcomes?', issue brief, The Commonwealth Fund, 30 January 2020, www.commonwealthfund.org/publications/issue-briefs/2020/jan/us-health-care-global-perspective-2019.

16 A. Merelli, 'Why Jeff Bezos, Warren Buffett, and Jamie Dimon gave up on their venture to disrupt US healthcare', *Quartz*, 7 January 2021, https://qz.com/1952225/why-amazon-berkshire-hathaway-and-jpmorgans-haven-failed/.

17 Warren Buffett, speaking at the Berkshire Hathaway annual shareholder meeting, 1 May 2021.

18 'Stagekings: the journey so far', https://www.stagekings.com.au/about.

19 B. Gates & M. Gates, 'Why we swing for the fences', 2020 Annual Letter, *GatesNotes*, 10 February 2020, www.gatesnotes.com/2020-Annual-Letter.

20 Author interview with Umit Subasi, 7 September 2021.

21 Author interview with Glenn Keys, 13 September 2021.

22 L. Freedman, *Strategy: A History*, Oxford University Press, Oxford, 2013.

23 A. Chandler, *Strategy and Structure: Chapters in the history of industrial enterprise*, Doubleday, New York, 1962.

24 M. Porter, 'What is strategy?', *Harvard Business Review*, November–December 1996.

25 H. Mintzberg, 'Crafting strategy', *Harvard Business Review*, July 1987.

26 M. Reeves, K. Haanæs & J. Sinha, *Your Strategy Needs a Strategy: How to choose and execute the right approach*, Harvard Business Review Press, Boston, Massachusetts, 2015. Also M. Reeves, K. & J. Sinha, 'Navigating the dozens of different strategy options', *Harvard Business Review*, 24 June 2015.

27 T.W. Malnight, I. Buche & C. Dhanaraj, 'Put purpose at the core of your strategy', *Harvard Business Review*, September–October 2019.

28 A. Gast, P. Illanes, N. Probst, B. Schaninger & B. Simpson, 'Purpose: shifting from why to how', *McKinsey Quarterly*, McKinsey.com, 22 April 2020.

29 Author interview with Natalie Simmons, 27 August 2021.

30 K. Tiffany, 'The rise and fall of an American tech giant', *The Atlantic*, July–August 2021.

31 Australian Centre for Business Growth, 'Lack of leadership and planning leading cause of small business failure: CEO study', media release, 20 November 2018, https://centreforbusinessgrowth.com/news-and-events/reasons-smes-fail/.

32 N. Nichols, 'The rise of Guzman y Gomez: The making of a global brand', *Business News Australia*, 1 April 2021, https://www.businessnewsaustralia.com/articles/the-rise-of-guzman-y-gomez--the-making-of-a-global-brand.html.

33 J.L. Gaddis, *On Grand Strategy*, Penguin Press, New York, 2018, p. 21.

34 C. Thompson, 'How the electric car became the future of transportation', *Insider*, PWC, 3 July 2017, https://www.businessinsider.com/electric-car-history-2017-5?r=AU&IR=T.

35 Electric Vehicle Council, *State of Electric Vehicles*, August 2021, https://electricvehiclecouncil.com.au/reports/state-of-electric-vehicles-2021/.

36 TripAdvisor, Travellers' Choice 2021, Best of the best, 'Best brunch spots – world', https://www.tripadvisor.co.uk/TravelersChoice-Restaurants-cBrunch. Also E. Jenne, 'The best restaurant for brunch in the whole world according to Tripadvisor is right here in London', *MyLondon*, 25 July 2021, https://www.mylondon.news/whats-on/whats-on-news/best-restaurant-brunch-whole-world-21128760.

37 J. Lutrario, 'Seven restaurant chains make Fast Track 100', *BigHospitality*, 3 December 2018, www.bighospitality.co.uk/Article/2018/12/03/Fast-Track-100-restaurants. Also R. Branson, 'Entrepreneurs are the lifeblood of UK business', Virgin.com, 17 December 2018, www.virgin.com/richard-branson/entrepreneurs-are-lifeblood-uk-business.

38 W. Isaacson, *The Innovators: How a group of hackers, geniuses and geeks created the digital revolution*, Simon & Schuster UK, London, 2015.

39 C. Walsh, 'Jobs, Einstein, and Franklin', *The Harvard Gazette*, Harvard Public Affairs and Communications, Cambridge, Massachusetts, 9 April 2013.

40 J.M. Keynes, *Newton, the Man*, lecture written for the Royal Society of London, 1946.

41 D.H. Pink, *Drive: the surprising truth about what motivates us*, Riverhead Books, New York, 2009.

42 D. Adams, *The Hitchhiker's Guide to the Galaxy*, The Folio Society, London, 2010.

43 A. Haldane, 'The creative economy', The Inaugural Glasgow School of Art Creative Engagement Lecture, The Glasgow School of Art, 22 November 2018, https://www.bankofengland.co.uk/-/media/boe/files/speech/2019/the-creative-economy-speech-by-andy-haldane.pdf.

44 C. Naughtin, 'Telehealth in Australia during COVID-19 and beyond: Insights', *CSIRO Algorithm*, 31 July 2020, https://algorithm.data61.csiro.au/telehealth-usage-in-australia-has-sky-rocketed/.

45 www.radiolamington.com.

46 J. Cleese, *Creativity: A short and cheerful guide*, Hutchinson, Random House UK, London, 2020.

47 Orange Sky Australia, 'Our story', https://orangesky.org.au/our-story/.

48 A. Toffler, *Future Shock*, Pan Books, London, 1970.

49 J. Cleese, *Creativity: A short and cheerful guide*, Hutchinson, Random House UK, London, 2020.

50 A. Beard, 'Drunk people are better at creative problem solving', *Harvard Business Review*, May–June 2018.

51 F. Kerr & L. Maze, *The Art & Science of Looking Up*, http://www.gliderglobal.com/wp-content/uploads//THE-ART-AND-SCIENCE-OF-LOOKING-UP-REPORT_2019.pdf.

52 Psychology Today, 'Creativity', https://www.psychologytoday.com/au/basics/creativity.

53 E. Catmull, *Creativity, Inc*, Bantam Press, London, 2014.

54 The J. Paul Getty Museum, 'Johann Friedrich Böttger', https://www.getty.edu/art/collection/artists/726/johann-friedrich-bottger-german-1682-1719/.

55 C. Jones, *Chuck Amuck: The life and times of an animated cartoonist*, Farrar, Straus and Giroux, New York, 1999.

56 J. Kindt, 'Friday essay: Secrets of the Delphic Oracle and how it speaks to us today', *The Conversation*, 22 July 2016.

57 *Cambridge Dictionary*, Cambridge University Press, Cambridge, 2021, https://dictionary.cambridge.org/dictionary/english/clarity.

58 T. Boyd, 'Westpac's New Operating Model', *Australian Financial Review*, 4 May 2021, https://www.afr.com/chanticleer/westpac-s-new-operating-model-20210503-p57of3 and 'Cost-cutting King wants to be Eight Billion-Dollar Man', *Australian Financial Review*, 3 May 2021, https://www.afr.com/chanticleer/cost-cutting-king-wants-to-be-eight-billion-dollar-man-20210503-p57oe3.

59 C. Zook, 'Desperately Seeking Simplicity', *Harvard Business Review*, Harvard Business School Publication Corporation, Boston, 2 February 2012.

60 T. Schwartz, 'The Power of Deceptive Simplicity', *Harvard Business Review*, Harvard Business School Publication Corporation, Boston, 25 April 2011.

61 Author interview with Suzanne Hopman, 10 September 2021.

62 Quoted in S.D. Anthony, A. Trotter, R.D. Bell & E.I. Schwartz, 'The Five Behaviors of Transformational Organizations', Innosight.com, October 2019, www.innosight.com/insight/the-five-behaviors-of-transformational-organizations.

63 Netflix, 'Long-term view', Netflix.com, https://ir.netflix.net/ir-overview/long-term-view/default.aspx.

64 B Lab, 'About B Corps', https://bcorporation.net/about-b-corps.

65 Author interview with Glenn Keys, 13 September 2021.

66 www.thechangecompany.com.au

67 MIT School of Management, 'Buzzword Strategy Generator', *The Strategic Agility Project, MIT Sloan Management Review*, https://sloanreview.mit.edu/article/buzzword-strategy-generator-are-you-developing-meaningful-strategies/.

68 R. Rumelt, *Good Strategy/Bad Strategy*, Profile Books, London, 2017.

69 M. Thatcher, Sir Robert Menzies Lecture, Monash University, Melbourne, 6 October 1981.

70 M. Wilkinson, 'What consensus really means', Facilitation blog, Managementhelp.org, 18 July 2013, https://managementhelp.org/blogs/facilitation/2013/07/18/what-consensus-really-means/.

71 Infrastructure Australia, *Reforms to meet Australia's future infrastructure needs: 2021 Australian infrastructure plan*, 2 September 2021, www.infrastructureaustralia.gov.au/publications/2021-australian-infrastructure-plan.

72 Committee for Sydney, 'Sydney Awards recognise decades of achievement, lifting up millions across the city and around the world', media release, 16 September 2021, https://sydney.org.au/news-events/media-release/sydney-awards-recognise-decades-of-achievement-lifting-up-millions-across-the-city-and-around-the-world/.

73 Author interview with Romilly Madew, 14 September 2021.

74 M. Anderson, Meeting Cartoon #5327, Andertoons, https://andertoons.com/meeting/cartoon/5327/we-all-agree-lets-go-back-to-desks-discuss-why-this-wont-work.

75 In S.J. Dubner, 'How to make meetings less terrible', *Freakonomics Radio*, episode 389, 18 September 2019, https://freakonomics.com/ podcast/meetings/.

76 J.B. Sørensen & G.R. Carroll, 'Why good arguments make better strategy', *MIT Sloan Management Review*, MIT Sloan School of Management, Cambridge, Massachusetts, 3 June 2021.

77 Author interview with Susan Coghill, 8 October 2021.

78 D&AD, 'Matesong' Graphite Pencil award, https://www.dandad. org/awards/professional/2020/231740/matesong/. Also The Caples Awards, 'M&C Saatchi, Tourism Australia, "Matesong"', https:// caples.org/2020-winners-results/?id=549&cat=PR.

79 Author interview with Susan Coghill, 8 October 2021.

80 Author interview with Umit Subasi, 7 September 2021.

81 C.R. Pierpont, 'The secret lives of Leonardo da Vinci', *The New Yorker*, 9 October 2017.

82 H. Mintzberg, 'Patterns in strategy formation', *Management Science*, vol. 24, no. 9, May 1978.

83 S. Kaplan, 'After searing tragedy, Everest's deadliest route is now off-limits', *The Washington Post*, 18 February 2015, https:// www.washingtonpost.com/news/morning-mix/wp/2015/02/18/ after-searing-tragedy-everests-deadliest-route-is-now-off-limits/.

84 W. Paddock & P. Paddock, *Famine, 1975! America's decision – who will survive?*, Little, Brown and Company, Boston, Massachusetts, 1967.

85 P. Ehrlich, *The Population Bomb*, Ballantine Books, New York, 1968.

86 L.S. Hardin, 'Bellagio 1969: The green revolution', *Nature*, vol. 455, pp. 470–471, 24 September 2008.

87 G. Shaw, 'How Lin-Manuel Miranda's non-stop work ethic from a young age made "Hamilton" one of the most successful musicals

of all time', *Business Insider Australia*, 22 December 2017, https://www.businessinsider.com.au/lin-manuel-miranda-work-ethic-hamilton-success-2017-12. Also J. Youshaei, 'Hamilton: How Lin-Manuel Miranda created a hit musical', Forbes, 24 November 2020, https://www.forbes.com/sites/jonyoushaei/2020/11/24/hamilton-how-lin-manuel-miranda-created-a-hit-musical/.

88 Bessemer Venture Partners, 'The Anti-Portfolio', www.bvp.com/anti-portfolio.

Index

Be better with business books

MAJOR STREET

We hope you enjoy reading this book. We'd love you to post a review on social media or your favourite bookseller site. Please include the hashtag #majorstreetpublishing.

Major Street Publishing specialises in business, leadership, personal finance and motivational non-fiction books. If you'd like to receive regular updates about new Major Street books, email info@majorstreet.com.au and ask to be added to our mailing list.

Visit majorstreet.com.au to find out more about our books (print, audio and ebooks) and authors, read reviews and find links to our Your Next Read podcast.

We'd love you to follow us on social media.

in linkedin.com/company/major-street-publishing

f facebook.com/MajorStreetPublishing

instagram.com/majorstreetpublishing

@MajorStreetPub